MARY JO'S
CUISINE

MARY JO'S
CUISINE

A Cookbook
By Mary Jo McMillin

ORANGE FRAZER PRESS
Wilmington, Ohio

ISBN 978-1933197-33-3
Copyright©2007 Mary Jo McMillin

Additional copies of *Mary Jo's Cuisine* may be ordered directly from:

Orange Frazer Press
P.O. Box 214
Wilmington, OH 45177

Telephone 1.800.852.9332 for price and shipping information.
Website: www.orangefrazer.com

Book design by Chad DeBoard
Cover design by Jeff Fulwiler

Library of Congress Cataloging-in-Publication Data

McMillin, Mary Jo, 1941-
Mary Jo's cuisine : a cookbook / by Mary Jo McMillin.
  p. cm.
ISBN 978-1-933197-33-3 (alk. paper)
  1. Cookery, French. 2. Mary Jo's Cuisine (Restaurant) I. Title.

TX719.M3967 2007
641.5941--dc22

2007003833

For my mother, Cleo, whose
vision and trust left me alone in
the kitchen.

ACKNOWLEDGEMENTS

I would like to thank my children, David and Catherine, who willingly ate their way through France and India during childhood when they longed for Kraft and Hostess. They guided me in the world of business and still find being together around the dinner table a family treasure. I'm grateful to Ballymaloe House and Ballymaloe Cookery School for decades of inspiration and affirmation. I thank James Reiss for his extraordinary editorial skill and encouragement in this writing life. I bow deeply in appreciation to my staff, purveyors, friends, and patrons who over the years supported my work and allowed me to have the only job I ever wanted.

TABLE OF CONTENTS

PREFACE

In July 1986 I rented the old White Cross Dairy across the street from Miami University in Oxford, Ohio. For more than a decade the space had been occupied by a pizza delivery service; there were inches of grease to scrape off the floor. I scrubbed and painted, invested my savings in a six-burner Garland gas range, a two-deck Blodgett baking oven, and, to get up to code, a large triple sink to accompany the reach-in cooler and stainless hood purchased from the pizza biz.

Mary Jo's Cuisine opened in September as a take-out shop offering freshly baked breads and pastries, soups, salads, stews, pastas, curries, and trays of hand-crafted party food, bringing the Oxford community a sampling of the best European provincial cooking and ethnic dishes. We began without a display case or dishwashing machine and made change out of a cash box.

From day one everything was made from scratch. After training in Ireland, I was determined to cook seasonally and buy from local growers. I purchased apples, squash, and potatoes from Owen's; strawberries and asparagus from Freels'; corn and tomatoes from Butterfield's; lamb and eggs from House's; and blackberries from Hacker's. Farmers and gardeners often came to the door, selling boxes of summer bounty — until jam, concentrated tomatoes, corn cut from cobs, and sliced peppers filled the freezer and storeroom. One summer I found morels growing in the brush out back, and each spring I gathered elder flowers behind the building to make lemon cordial. Frozen bags of saved shrimp shells became the base for seafood bisque every few months. I was never willing to follow trends. I stayed with classic country cooking and authentic culinary offerings from all over the world.

Tucked behind a circular drive around a wooded lawn, the green-shuttered shop resembled a fairy-tale house. The white stone front looked inviting, with geranium- and alyssum-filled window boxes in summer and wreaths in winter. Summer shade came from the nearby catalpa, hackberry, and wild cherry trees, while ceiling fans offered "Natural Air-Conditioning Inside."

In January of the first year, I bought five tables and painted some cast-off classroom chairs pink. I unpacked boxes of hand-thrown Irish pottery, arranged rummage-sale vases of fresh flowers, and opened for a simple soup-and-salad luncheon. In May I added five more tables and extended the menu to include quiches, composed salads, and hot entrees. A brisk lunch trade followed — for seventeen years.

By 1993 I felt ready to include weekend French country dinners from a fixed-price menu similar to the gourmet-to-go dinners I had catered for years. I knew we needed wine to succeed with dinner. It's illegal to allow patrons to carry in alcoholic beverages in Ohio, and a drink permit would demand a full year of wrangling plus a steep annual fee and a sizable increase in liability insurance.

After months of letter writing, neighborhood campaigning, vowing discretion to my Presbyterian landladies, and convincing state officials that the population of our town had grown enough to release another permit, I was granted a license on one last condition. The state demanded a urinal be installed in the men's room. The newly remodeled, spacious ladies' lav, the only place large enough for a urinal, became the men's to accommodate the porcelain pissoir—all this for a cozy café with thirty seats! Due to its odd placement, the fixture was cleaned yet seldom noticed after its debut-toasting with rounds of sparkling wine. Now that we had proper toilets, the state of Ohio granted Mary Jo's Cuisine a liquor license, and we began to serve Sonoma-Cutrer, Au Bon Climat, and Veuve Cliquot with our weekend dinners.

From coast to coast, parents and university visitors arrived—Nance's dad called us his "favorite New York restaurant." Cincinnati and Dayton newspapers cheered us on. *Ohio, Cincinnati,* and *City Beat* were on our team. Food luminary Darina Allen visited from Ireland and heaped praise in the *Irish Examiner. Gourmet* magazine never showed up, but our clientele knew they were dining as well as patrons at Chez Panisse in the Bay Area.

"It smells so good in here" was a constant refrain as the front door's macramé bells announced another arrival. From the open cooking area beside the dining room, anyone walking in could smell sautéing onions, wine-scented stews, bubbling tomato sauce, and spicy masalas—while the ovens turned out chocolate cakes, oatmeal cookies, fruit tarts, and breads, breads, breads.

Steve and his son Mark repaired the fridges, sometimes at midnight or on Christmas Day. An uptown florist traded slices of chocolate cake for blown roses. When Dan came in every day to collect food scraps for his hens, he listened to my woes and occasionally changed the florescent bulbs. One Saturday night a local big shot bet another high roller $10, 000; this ended up with a grown man dancing among stemmed wine glasses atop one of my white linen-draped tables.

Toni once told me it was unbelievable dining out knowing Mary Jo would actually be there cooking and plating dinners. My restaurant wasn't a place where a chef supervised and cooks sautéed. It was as if you were going to dinner at a friend's house; only, your friend stayed at the stove while you dipped crusts of her baguettes into pools of sauce Bourguignon.

During a jam-packed graduation weekend the ancient bathroom plumbing needed to be dug up by a backhoe, and the landladies had to bring in gaudy portapotties. JR engaged the health inspector in long conversations about music, so we could get on with lunch. Jim drove up from Cincinnati for a solitary gentleman's repast every Wednesday. Schuette had his gin on the rocks right after he took his seat. Dave and Alice never left a crumb on their plates. World-travelers Judith and Roger seldom missed a menu. L and G spoke French and sipped champagne.

As time passed Miami took over catering university events, and fewer people wanted to work. Three strong women who stayed with me over the last seasons were a godsend. After nearly eighteen years of eighty-plus pressured hours a week, no sick days, and no one to follow in my footsteps, I cut back lunch and focused on three nights of dinner a week.

When I was approached with an opportunity to sell, I didn't feel I had the energy to teach another student how to set a table. The health department was insisting on five thousand dollars' worth of new equipment I didn't need. Perhaps my time had come. Three entrepreneurs with deep pockets and a "business plan" would tap into the college-town scene with low food costs, glam refurbishment, and a large bar built in the back store room. They wanted none of my "intellectual property," just the opportunity to acquire the location and the drink license I had squeezed from Liquor Control. The deal was fair. I wouldn't have to invest thousands in a new fire-suppression system. I knew I'd run my course.

At first it felt good to think I wouldn't have to spend the summer writing a new wine list, planning menus, and trying to find workers. I wouldn't be paying the hefty insurance premium, standing in dread of the health inspector, and having to check the fridge thermometers every day.

The house was packed during the final weeks, and we had a gala garden party for friends and colleagues on the last Sunday. I spent three weeks boxing up my pots, knives, and books. I cleaned shelves, scrubbed floors, and dug up clumps of thyme. On the eve of the final walk-through, I nicked the mortar in a hall and drank champagne with two friends before we threw our glasses into the bushes out back.

My phone number was wiped out. I saw my window boxes removed, my sign taken down. It was hard to let go—a huge part of me felt missing. It was time to share these recipes.

Before you begin, I'd like to ask you to invest in a good scale and a sharp chef's knife. Most of the world cooks by weight. For some reason, Americans stuff food into cups, unfortunately with little accuracy. As I've tested these recipes at home, I've used assorted measuring cups and spoons, only to find the measurements seldom equal.

A scale will speed up measuring. It is far faster to lump items on and off a scale than it is to chop and measure in cups. Buy a scale that clearly marks gradations up to ¼ ounce. A scale is not expensive and will transform your approach to cooking. I use a precision scale that weighs only up to two pounds but easily shows fractions of ounces. For liquids, fluid ounces, use glass or plastic measuring cups with clearly marked increments.

Teach yourself to hone your chopping knife daily, and locate a reliable sharpening service to touch up the edge once a year. There are many fine French, German, and Japanese knives on the market, but excellent knives manufactured by the Chicago Cutlery Company are available in hardware stores.

Two ingredients used repeatedly may not be common in most kitchens. One is fresh chili, which gives a spicy lift without being strong. During the summer I use the green and red cayenne peppers that grow in my garden, and during the winter I select serrano chilis in the supermarket. Chili measurements in the recipes include the seeds, are minimal, and may be increased, decreased, or omitted according to taste. Another spice to look for is Ceylon cinnamon or canela. This delicate cinnamon, true cinnamon (Cinnamomum zeylanicum), is a kinder food companion than the strong cassia cinnamon (Cinnamomum cassia, "apple pie cinnamon") standard in the United States. Ceylon cinnamon is readily found in a supermarket's Mexican section or in a specialty spice catalog. Ceylon cinnamon is preferred in Western Europe and throughout Latin America. It is sold in multi-layered coils and is easy to use in wide splinters or broken segments.

This book presents many of *Mary Jo's Cuisine's* favorites designed for the home kitchen. I've been mindful of working with ingredients that can be found in small cities across this country. Most recipes are adjusted to yield between four and eight servings.

My continual advice is to taste, taste, taste, as you teach yourself to season. If a soup or sauce seems bland, lift the flavor. Always at hand for last-minute boosts, my "spice box" components include sea salt, freshly ground pepper, freshly grated nutmeg, fresh lemon or lime juice, finely chopped chili, and fresh herbs in season. Rely on your own preferences and create memorable flavor. Enjoy!

—Mary Jo

MARY JO'S
CUISINE

SOUPS

The following soups are all puréed. They do not demand a lot of chopping and are quick to prepare. The method is similar for all the soups.

Time and again I was asked, "Are your soups cream-based?" This question always baffled me; it would be too expensive to use cream as a soup base. My soups have puréed potato, rice, or soft vegetables, which give a creamy texture, and a little cream or milk enriches the flavor. This last fillip may be omitted, but please sweat the vegetables in butter. There's no need to peel and chop garlic; in puréed soups the peelings disappear. Most of these soups call for chicken stock, though vegetarian stock may always be substituted.

Everywhere I look there is soup from a can, soup from a frozen base; I start to fear there is very little honest homemade soup on our tables anymore. Soup before dinner tempers the appetite, and soup for lunch offers moderate calories for maximum satisfaction. I always knew that a basket of good bread and cups of stellar soup, brought to the table as soon as orders came in, kept our diners content.

Soup is easy, affordable, and provides welcome leftovers. My motto: Save The Soup.

BASIC CHICKEN STOCK

I can't imagine being without stock. The canned version may be used, but once you've discovered the rich flavor of homemade stock, you will always find a way to keep it on hand. The best stock is made with a whole chicken (Poached Chicken for Salad, p. 41); however, good stock may be made with chicken parts or even with the leftover carcass from Sunday's roast. Keep a bag in the freezer for necks, gizzards, chicken trimmings, and carcasses from roast chicken. Do not include livers. When you have a bundle and the day is cool, make a pot of stock.

Choose a deep soup pot that will hold 3- to 5-pounds chicken for stock (chicken parts are not as easy to poach for salad, because they tend to overcook, but if that is what you have to work with and you want to retrieve the nice chunks of meat, mind them carefully). Add sliced onion, celery, carrot, parsley, bay leaf, bits of garlic, a good pinch of thyme, black peppercorns, and barely cover with water. Add 1 rounded teaspoon of salt only if you are cooking the chicken for chicken salad; otherwise, simmer the stock without salt.

Bring the pot quickly to a boil, reduce heat to low, and simmer covered until the chicken is cooked through, 20–30 minutes for pieces. Remove chicken from the broth to a baking tray and allow to cool until you can pull off the large segments of breast and thigh/leg meat. Return the skin, bones, and bits to the stockpot. Continue to simmer for an additional 1–2 hours. Pull the reserved meat into salad-sized chunks and refrigerate when cool.

Remove stockpot from heat, uncover, and allow to stand until no longer scalding hot. Pour or ladle stock through a colander to remove vegetables and bones. Strain stock through a sieve. Place in plastic containers and cool to room temperature, uncovered, before refrigerating. This amount should make 2 quarts of rich-tasting stock.

For the best preservation, leave fat intact until ready to use stock. Once stock is fully chilled, fat forms a protective cap and will easily lift off. Homemade stock will keep 3 to 4 days in the coldest part of the fridge, or it may be chilled, degreased, and frozen in pint cartons or ziplock bags. For longer refrigerator storage, remove fat cap, bring the stock to a boil, cool to room temperature, cover, and return to the fridge.

POTATO SOUP AND VARIATIONS

The world loves potato soup: hot in winter, cold as Vichyssoise in summer; we made potato soup every week and always ran out. Choose Yukon Gold, russet, or white potatoes; do not use red-skinned potatoes, which are too sweet.

1 oz. (2 tablespoons) butter
12 oz. (3 cups sliced) onion
2 large branches celery, sliced (1½ cups)
2–3 whole cloves garlic
3–4 slices fresh green chili (optional)
1 lb. potatoes, peeled and cubed (3 generous cups)
32 fl. oz. (4 cups) chicken stock
16 fl. oz. (2 cups) water
4 fl. oz. (½ cup) cream or 8 fl. oz. (1 cup) half-and-half or whole milk
salt, white pepper, and freshly grated nutmeg to taste

1. Melt butter in soup pot or deep saucepan, add onion, celery, garlic, and chili; cover with butter papers,* reduce heat, and sweat at least 10 minutes or until vegetables are limp and translucent but not browned. Add potato, chicken stock, water, and good pinch of salt. Cover and boil gently 10–15 minutes or until potato is very tender.

2. Remove from heat; add cream or milk, and cool briefly. Purée 2–3 cups at a time in blender. Pour puréed soup into sieve and rub through with back of small ladle to remove any celery strings. Season to taste with salt and freshly ground pepper, sometimes a grating of nutmeg. Thin soup with a little water or milk if it seems too thick. Serve with sprinkling of freshly chopped parsley, chives, or mint. Makes 2 quarts.

VARIATIONS:

Cabbage Potato Soup: Increase butter to 2 oz. (4 tablespoons), reduce potato to 8 oz. When potato is almost cooked, add 12 oz. (4 packed cups) chopped green Savoy cabbage leaves, ribs removed. Cook steadily uncovered (to preserve green color) 10 minutes or until cabbage is tender. Add cream, and purée as directed. Use coarse sieve or purée only. Be sure to include nutmeg in cabbage variation.

Roasted Garlic Potato Soup: Wrap bulb of garlic in foil, roast until tender alongside whatever is going in oven. Add 8–10 cloves roasted garlic to sweating onions for Potato Soup.

Sorrel Soup: Add 4–6 oz. (2–3 cups) chopped sorrel leaves (or a mixture of sorrel and spinach) to soup during last minutes of cooking. Purée and finish as directed.

Vichyssoise: Chill Potato Soup, add 4–6 fl. oz. additional cream (½–¾ cup), salt, freshly ground pepper to taste, and serve with chopped chives.

* Butter papers: I've been the laughing stock of waves of young people as I've asked them to please save the waxed paper butter wrappers. These buttery papers are ideal to cover sweating vegetables; otherwise, use sheets of expensive waxed paper.

STAFF

*I*n *the early days I never had to worry about staff. Located across the street from the
university, I had a steady stream of applicants and a spindle of resumés on my desk.
One terrific young team came through like a spell of good weather, and as they moved on
one by one, the forecast changed. For a while I knew Todd could take over the stove and
Erin could run the front. Rolly mopped, John rolled pasta, Amy tirelessly mixed salad
after salad. Diane came in when I was certain there was no one to be found.*

*Jodie arrived as a freshman seeking work experience for a class project and returned as
staff throughout her college years. When she graduated and walked out as a foodie, she
went to work for Carlos and Charlie Trotter's in Chicago until, fed up with the city, she
decided to get closer to the heartland and returned to Oxford. I welcomed her back with
a salaried job and benefits as best I could manage. I envisioned her one day taking over
the business. Our first year together we increased lunch and added a Thursday "Bistro
Night." When Jodie fantasized remodeling and I opposed the idea, fearing the expense,
she was disheartened. By now she was isolated from the university scene. She needed
to return to the wider world. While I plated thousands of dinners after she left, I lifted
lettuce leaves higher, tucked the asparagus up closer to the salmon and the spuds, and
pooled the beurre blanc in a glistening stream as Jodie had learned in the city.*

*When I began serving luncheon, I hired Josette from Luxembourg and Pascale from
Belgium. Their French accents and knowledge of European food were a continual boon.
Pascale bowed out for years when her two children were born, but she stayed with me
until the last glass was poured — by then her daughter had a driver's license.*

In the back room forever washing lettuce, cutting vegetables, making vinaigrette, and puréeing soup, an older crew worried about our daughters in college. We gossiped about school affairs and anguished over the Iraq war. Pat worked at the local middle-school cafeteria and moonlighted for me in the late afternoons. Her steady calm sustained me through long evenings of jointing chickens, boning shoulders of lamb, and rolling pastry.

When I was convinced that students were willing only to answer the phone and run the register, in walked a young woman with a vibrant smile. Michelle swore she would memorize the wine list by the next day and insisted I hire her. She bought a black dress to make herself look slimmer. She came to work an hour early to crease the napkins and polish the glasses, as she recited the ingredients in the tomato bisque and the method for making a velouté. She bubbled with thank-yous, entertained the guests with her plans to work in Australia, and sold lots of wine.

Another Pat, Pat H., brought the flair of clipped Yorkshire speech and a Brit's keen wit. The golden bonus of her exceptional talent in the front of the house came with her abiding respect for our food and our mission. Plus, "Ya know, the tips felt damn good in the pocket."

CARROT SOUP/CARROT GINGER SOUP

My children grew up on this one. Even in their thirties they ask for carrot soup when they come home. Omit the cinnamon, ginger, and chili for children; add the spices for more mature palates.

1½ oz. (3 tablespoons) butter
1 3-inch by ½-inch strip Ceylon cinnamon, canela, or
  ½-inch cinnamon stick (optional)
1/16 teaspoon turmeric, a knife point (optional)
1 large, 10–12 oz., (3 cups) onion, peeled and sliced
1 large rib celery sliced, 3 oz. (¾ cup)
3 or 4 slices fresh chili or pinch of crushed red chilis (optional)
2–3 cloves garlic, smashed
1¼ lbs. (5 cups) carrots, peeled and sliced
1–2 tablespoons finely grated fresh ginger (optional)
24 fl. oz. (3 cups) chicken stock
8 fl. oz. (1 cup) water
½ teaspoon sugar (optional—if carrots lack sweetness)
salt to taste
4 fl. oz. (½ cup) half-and-half or milk with cream
freshly grated nutmeg

1. Melt butter in deep saucepan; add cinnamon and turmeric. Add sliced onions, celery, chili, garlic, and carrots. Toss to coat with butter; cover with butter papers and gently sweat 10–15 minutes or until onions are translucent and carrots are almost tender.

2. Stir in ginger, salt, optional sugar; add chicken stock and water. Cover and simmer soup steadily for 15 minutes or until carrots are very tender.

3. Remove from heat; fish out cinnamon pieces. Add cream or milk and allow to cool a few minutes. Purée in blender 2–3 cups at a time; pour soup through sieve, pressing out any vegetable lumps. Correct seasoning, adding more salt, pepper, sugar, and a grating of fresh nutmeg to taste. Serve warm with a sprinkling of fresh mint, chives, or parsley. Makes about 2 quarts.

This soup is delicious served chilled but will need more seasoning and could be thinned with a little water, stock, or cream.

ASPARAGUS SOUP

In spring our dinners often included both asparagus soup and asparagus as the green vegetable for the evening. When it was abundant and fresh from a local farm, there was nothing on the market that could come close to asparagus. Soup can be made with tender stalks alone, if you prefer to serve the tips separately; or, the tips may be cut off, blanched, and added to the soup after it is puréed. Collect chive flowers for a garnish.

1 oz. (2 tablespoons) butter
12 oz. (1 very large) onion, peeled and sliced
1 large green celery rib with leaves, sliced
2–3 cloves garlic, smashed
6 oz. potato (1 medium), peeled and diced (Yukon Gold or white)
16 fl. oz. (2 cups) chicken stock
24 fl. oz. (3 cups) water
18 oz. thinly sliced tender asparagus spears (4½ cups) asparagus tips blanched
    and reserved
4 fl. oz. (½ cup) half-and-half or ¼ cup cream and ¼ cup milk
salt and white pepper

1. Melt butter in soup pot. Add onion, celery, garlic; cover with butter papers and gently sweat until onion is translucent and tender, about 10 minutes.

2. Add diced potato, stock, water, salt; cover and boil gently until potato is tender.

3. Remove lid, raise heat, add sliced asparagus, and cook uncovered quickly until asparagus is tender. Keep lid off to preserve color.

4. Remove from heat; add cream, and purée 2–3 cups at a time in blender. Rub soup through sieve to remove any stringy bits. Season to taste with salt and freshly ground white pepper. Stir in reserved, cooked, and sliced asparagus tips before serving. Serve hot or chilled. Makes about 2 quarts.

MUSHROOM SOUP

Mushroom Soup secret: The soup will have more mushroom flavor if the mushrooms have gone a bit brown and shriveled in the fridge.

1½ oz. (3 tablespoons) butter
½ lb. (2 cups) onion, peeled and finely chopped
2 cloves garlic, finely chopped
3–4 thin slices fresh chili, finely chopped (optional)
1 lb. (6 cups) mushrooms, thinly sliced (may use processor)
24 fl. oz. (3 cups) chicken stock
1 tablespoon finely chopped fresh tarragon or 1 teaspoon dry tarragon
salt and freshly ground white pepper
24 fl. oz. (3 cups) whole milk thickened to a thin white sauce with
1½oz. (3 tablespoons) roux*
2 fl. oz. (¼ cup) heavy cream (optional but recommended)
few drops fresh lemon juice

1. Gently sweat onions and garlic in butter until very tender, 15–20 minutes.

2. Raise heat, stir in mushrooms, and cook until they begin to sauté. Add chicken stock, bring to simmer, cover and cook briefly until mushrooms flavor broth, 15 minutes.

3. Meanwhile, prepare thin white sauce: Bring milk to simmer and crumble in roux, whisking quickly and cook until it becomes consistency of cream. Immediately add hot white sauce to mushroom broth. (If white sauce waits, it will form a skin that will fleck the soup.)

4. Add heavy cream, fresh tarragon, or crumbled dry tarragon. Purée soup lightly in blender or use an immersion blender to break up mushroom slices.

5. Taste for seasonings, adding a few drops of lemon juice, freshly ground white pepper, and more salt if needed to lift flavor. Makes about 2 quarts.

For restaurant-style presentation, float ½ teaspoon lightly whipped cream on top of each cup of soup; dust with finely chopped parsley. When the soup comes to the table, the cream will have melted into a lacy froth.

*Roux is a cooked fat and starch compound used to thicken sauces. Roux here refers to a butter and flour mixture; however, it may be made with olive oil, bacon, or duck drippings. To make 2 oz. roux, melt l oz. (2 tablespoons) butter and whisk in 1 oz. (approximately ¼ cup) all-purpose flour. It is important to be aware that different flours give different results. If you use unbleached all-purpose flour, you will need less than if you use a lighter bleached all-purpose flour.

As the roux cooks, it should look like thick sour cream or soft fudge in the bottom of the pan. If it is too liquid, add a bit more flour; if the roux becomes a crumbly lump in the pan, add more butter. Stir over low heat 2–4 minutes to cook the flour.

Roux is a handy item to have in the fridge or freezer. Consider making up ¼ lb. (1 stick) butter and 4–4½ oz. (1 cup) flour. Roux will keep three weeks in the fridge or months in the freezer.

Butternut Squash Soup

Often called Mary Jo's best soup, gallon after gallon of Butternut Squash Soup lined our fridge from October through December. This was always the soup for our Thanksgiving Dinner.

1¾–2 lbs. butternut squash or other orange-fleshed winter squash should give 1¼ lbs. peeled, cubed squash (a generous quart)

1 oz. (2 tablespoons) butter

1½ inch Ceylon cinnamon, canela, or ½-inch stick cinnamon

6 oz. (1½ cups) onion, peeled and sliced (1 medium onion)

3 oz. (1 medium carrot) carrot, peeled and sliced

3 oz. (1-2 ribs) celery, sliced

2–3 whole cloves garlic, smashed

¼ teaspoon chopped fresh red chili, or pinch crushed red pepper

1 oz. (2 tablespoons) fresh ginger, peeled and finely grated

½ teaspoon garam masala*

³⁄₈ teaspoon turmeric

12 fl. oz. (1½ cups) chicken stock

20 fl. oz. (2½ cups) water

1 teaspoon salt

1 teaspoon brown sugar (optional)

4 fl. oz. (½ cup) cream, half-and-half, or whole milk

freshly grated nutmeg

1. To prepare squash, cut off ends, slice into 1-inch circles. Scoop out seeds, peel off rind with paring knife, and cut squash into large cubes. Set aside.

2. Heat butter in large soup pot; add cinnamon, then toss in sliced onions, carrots, celery, chili, and garlic. Cover with butter papers and sweat vegetables over gentle heat 10–20 minutes or until carrots are limp and tender, but not brown.

3. Add grated ginger, garam masala, turmeric, and stir until fragrant. Mix in prepared squash; add chicken stock, water, and salt; cover and bring to a boil. Simmer steadily until squash and carrots are very tender, 15–20 minutes.

4. Cool slightly, fish out cinnamon sticks, and add cream. Purée soup 2–3 cups at a time in blender and use small ladle to swirl soup through strainer to remove celery strings and chili seeds. Correct seasonings, adding salt, freshly ground white pepper, brown sugar, and freshly grated nutmeg to taste. Thin to desired consistency with water, stock or milk. Makes 2 quarts.

* Garam Masala (an Indian spice blend)

1 small nutmeg, broken with side of chef's knife
1½ tablespoons whole green cardamom, including husk
2 tablespoons crumbled Ceylon cinnamon or I broken cinnamon stick
1 tablespoon whole cloves
½ tablespoon black peppercorns

Roast spices in dry iron skillet until fragrant. Cool slightly and grind to powder in spice grinder. Sift and store in small jar with tight fitting lid. Makes scant ½ cup.

Note: To clean a spice grinder, add a handful of white rice. Grind and discard the rice. Do not try to wash a spice grinder. An electric coffee mill makes an excellent spice grinder.

Tomato Bisque

Always best with fresh tomatoes. In winter when we used canned tomatoes, we lifted the flavor with a speck of ground allspice.

1 oz. (2 tablespoons) butter

3 splinters Ceylon cinnamon, canela, or ½-inch cinnamon stick

1 large onion (8–10 oz.) (2 cups), peeled and sliced

1 large rib celery, sliced (¾ cup)

2 large whole cloves garlic, smashed

¼ teaspoon sliced fresh chili or ⅛ scant teaspoon crushed red chilis

½ teaspoon paprika

2 lbs. very ripe Italian tomatoes* chunked or 2 15 oz. cans plum tomatoes

1 tablespoon white rice

16 fl. oz. (2 cups) chicken stock

sprig of fresh thyme, oregano, or basil (or pinch dry thyme or tarragon)

½ teaspoon sugar

1 teaspoon salt

freshly ground pepper to taste

fresh basil in season

2 fl. oz. (¼ cup) heavy cream

1. Warm cinnamon in melted butter and toss in sliced onion, celery, garlic, and chili. Cover with butter papers and sweat gently about 10 minutes, or until vegetables are limp, reduced, and tender. Stir in paprika and sauté a few seconds.

2. Cut unpeeled fresh tomatoes in half around equator. Squeeze out and save seedy centers. Run seedy juice through sieve. Discard seeds; add juice to soup. Stir in tomatoes, rice, and chicken stock. (With canned tomatoes, an additional cup of water may be needed.) Season with sugar and salt; add 2 sprigs basil, thyme, or oregano or pinch of dry thyme or tarragon. Cover and simmer steadily until rice is mushy 20–30 minutes, stirring occasionally to make sure rice doesn't stick on bottom of pan.

3. Just before puréeing and sieving soup, remove cinnamon splinters and herb stems. Purée soup in blender and run through sieve to remove tomato skins and seeds. Add heavy cream (to stay on the safe side of curdling, use only heavy cream in tomato soup. Freeze remaining cream in ice-cube trays, store in plastic bag, and save for other soups.) Taste for seasonings adding salt, sugar, and perhaps pinch of allspice. Makes 2 quarts.

* Sometimes commercially canned tomatoes are processed with citric acid, which makes them retain firmness. These tomatoes need to be puréed in a blender before cooking them in the soup.

North Pole

O ur venerable, thirty-foot Kolpack reach-in cooler held hundreds of dollars in produce, meats, dairy, and hundreds of work hours in soup, sauces, and pastries. I glanced at the temperature gauges above the six-inch thick doors every few minutes and kept my ear on the hum of the compressor. Sometimes I'd drive to the shop in the middle of the night just to check the fridges. A power outage was a nightmare and a breakdown a scene of panic. Stickers with North Pole's phone number were always in sight.

Before one big graduation dinner – with temperatures rising into the nineties, no air-conditioning, and my fridge thermometer dangerously close to 50°F – rescue tumbled from the North Pole truck. "It ain't tore up yet," Steve murmured as a shot of freon and the twist of a few wires brought back the motor's purr and the thermometer's downward spiral.

Sporting his Clark Gable mustache and starched white shirt, Steve claimed he'd earned his wrinkles and specs. His pride and joy was a mint "fitty-five" bronze Chevy. He'd had Mark at his side ever since the tyke could tinker with tools. He'd championed Mark through a motorcycle racing career and believed in him when the restless lad with flowing locks partied through vocational school. After Mark married his blonde sweetheart, he settled down as Steve's right-hand man.

Their empire grew to include vast commercial refrigeration contracts. They were on call weekends, holidays, nights – they never took vacations. We lost Steve early to cancer; Mark carried on.

I'd listen, spellbound, as he groused about the IRS and mentioned cash deals for fast cars. We bonded over taxes and red tape. As small businesses, we felt squashed – corporate America was taking over.

GAZPACHO

Don't even consider making this until high summer when tomatoes are deep red and dead ripe; then make it every day until you get your fill for the year.

2 lbs. (4 cups) ripe chunked summer tomatoes
¼ cup finely diced sweet onion
1 large clove garlic mashed to a paste with ½ teaspoon salt
¼ teaspoon green or red chili with seeds, chopped (optional)
1½ tablespoons red wine vinegar
¼ teaspoon ground cumin
1 tablespoon olive oil
salt and pepper or Tabasco sauce to taste

1. There is no need to peel or seed tomatoes for gazpacho. Just core, remove any blemishes, and chunk. Place onion, crushed garlic, and chili in bottom of blender jar. Add ¼ tomatoes. Pulse and blend to form thick juice. Add remaining tomatoes and blend to purée. Press purée through sieve to remove seeds and bits of skin.

2. To this soup base, add red wine vinegar, cumin, and olive oil. Add salt and pepper or Tabasco sauce to taste. Chill seasoned soup base (there will be 1 quart or 4 cups of base) for at least 2 hours or up to 2 days. Shortly before serving add all or some of the following:

1 large peeled, seeded, diced tomato*
¼ peeled, seeded, diced cucumber
¼ diced green, red, or yellow sweet pepper
¼ cup finely chopped sweet onion or scallions
chopped fresh basil, mint, cilantro, or parsley

Serve chilled with crusty peasant bread. Makes 6 cups.

* To peel and seed a tomato: Loosen skin of vine-ripened fruit by drawing the flat side of a paring knife up and over the tomato's extremity; core and remove skin in ribbons. Alternatively scald tomato 10–20 seconds in boiling water or spear tomato on carving fork and turn in gas flame until skin splits. Cut in half at the equator, turn each half upside down, and squeeze out seedy bits or lift out seed pockets with a finger.

Note: Gazpacho base without olive oil makes a refreshing raw tomato juice for drinks.

CHILLED CUCUMBER SOUP

Here's reason enough to make your own yogurt. I felt almost guilty selling this soup, it was so easy to put together.

3–4 slicing cucumbers, or 1½ lbs. seedless cucumbers
1 clove garlic, sliced and crushed to a paste with ½ teaspoon salt
½ (1 teaspoon) small green chili, finely chopped (optional)
¾ cup thinly sliced green onion
16 fl. oz. (2 cups) plain whole milk yogurt, homemade if possible*
2 fl. oz. (¼ cup) cream or sour cream (optional)
1 tablespoon white wine vinegar
½ tablespoon lemon juice
¼ teaspoon ground cumin
1–2 tablespoons olive oil (optional)
salt and freshly ground pepper to taste
finely chopped fresh mint, dill, or parsley

1. Peel cucumbers, slice lengthwise, and scoop out seeds with teaspoon. Place seeds along with ⅓ cup water in blender; whiz to fine purée; press through sieve and use this cucumber water in soup. You should have at least 1 cup. If using seedless or English cucumbers, omit this step, and add ¾–1 cup of cold water to diced cucumbers.

2. Cut cucumber halves into strips, then large dice (measure a generous quart). In mixing bowl combine cucumber, crushed garlic (use tip of your knife on wooden board to crush garlic and salt), chili, and green onion.

3. Coarsely purée mixture in blender in batches, adding cucumber water. Leave last 2 cups of cucumber mixture in blender. Add yogurt plus optional cream and pulse once on and off to mix. Combine puréed mixtures. Rinse out blender jar with 2 tablespoons water and add to soup. Season with white wine vinegar, lemon juice, cumin, salt and pepper. Chill and serve with fresh mint, dill, or parsley. Makes about 6 cups.

* To make yogurt you will need whole milk and a plain, natural, pectin-free—organic if possible—yogurt to begin. Yogurt may be made with low-fat milk, but it's never as nice. Yogurt is milk in its most digestible form and will stay fresh for weeks in refrigerated sealed glass jars.

Rinse a deep saucepan with cold water and add 1 quart milk. Bring to a boil over moderate heat, stirring from time to time, until the milk foams and rises in the pan. Remove pan from heat and cool milk to lukewarm, about 118°F—you should be able to hold your clean little finger in the milk up to the count of 10. While waiting for the milk to cool, prepare 2 sterilized pint glass jars each containing a rounded tablespoon of yogurt culture. This can be purchased yogurt or yogurt left from your last batch.

Pour warm milk, tested with your clean finger, into the jars. Stir to combine with the yogurt culture. Cover tightly with plastic wrap; nestle the jars in terry towels inside a small thermal plastic picnic box; cover and set aside 4–12 hours or until set. The setting time will depend on the warmth of the container. In summer yogurt will set in an afternoon; in winter it can take half a day or longer. When ready the yogurt will be firm in the jar, and there will be a thin layer of watery liquid on top. Store in the refrigerator, and continue the process, using your own yogurt as the starter, which will stay active for years if used regularly.

CHILLED CURRIED PEA SOUP

This cooked, puréed and chilled soup is surprisingly simple because it uses frozen peas. We poured Curried Pea and Chilled Carrot Ginger soups side by side into cold cups for our gala tasting menu at the end of our season each June.

½ oz. (1 tablespoon) butter
2 tablespoons olive oil
5 oz. (1 cup) onion (1 medium), peeled and chopped
3 oz. (¾ cup) thinly sliced celery
2 cloves garlic, peeled and sliced
3–4 teaspoons curry powder
½ teaspoon garam masala (p.13)
1 teaspoon salt
16 fl. oz. (2 cups) chicken stock
16 fl. oz. (2 cups) water
1 lb. frozen peas (4 cups)
4 oz. (½ cup) sour cream
4 oz. (½ cup) plain whole milk yogurt (preferably homemade—p.21)

1. Heat butter and olive oil in medium soup pot, gently sweat onion and celery until tender and translucent. Add garlic, curry powder, garam masala and stir until spices are fragrant. Add salt, stock, and water; cover and simmer 10 minutes.

2. Add peas and simmer 10 minutes longer until peas are tender. Cool slightly. Purée soup in 2 batches in blender. (Taste soup and make a decision about texture. I always run this soup through a sieve to remove the pea hulls, but this is totally a matter of preference.) Leave 2 cups of soup in blender; add sour cream, yogurt and pulse once to mix. Pour batches together and taste for seasoning. Remember that a chilled soup always needs more salt than one served warm. Makes 6 cups.

Corn And Pepper Soup

I couldn't believe this soup when I first tasted it. The creamy sweetness of fresh corn plus the fruitiness of ripe pepper combine for one of summer's best flavors. Serve this soup warm or cold with a dusting of chives and nasturtium petals.

½ oz. (1 tablespoon) butter
1 medium onion (6 oz., 1½ cups sliced)
1 large red or yellow pepper (6-7 oz., 1½ cups sliced)
1 large clove garlic, peeled and sliced
⅛-¼ teaspoon sliced fresh chili
3 full ears sweet corn (bicolor recommended)
16 fl. oz. (2 cups) chicken stock
8 fl. oz. (1 cup) water
2 fl. oz. (¼ cup) cream (optional)
salt, white pepper

1. Melt butter in medium soup pot. Add sliced onion, pepper, garlic, and chili; sweat over low heat until vegetables are limp.

2. Meanwhile, shuck corn and rub off silk. Using a very sharp, small knife, cut off corn kernels over a bowl. (Cut through the middle of the corn kernels, taking care not to cut into the kernel heads or nibs.) Scrape cobs with knife blade to extract remaining pulp. Keep cobs. You should have at least 12 oz. or 2 cups cut and scraped corn.

3. Add stock, water, and ½ teaspoon salt to onions and pepper. Bring to boil. Add cobs; cover and cook cobs in onion broth for 10 minutes. Remove cobs with tongs. Allow cobs to cool until they can be handled. Again scrape cobs with small knife blade to remove remaining pulp. Discard cobs.

4. Add corn kernels and pulp to broth and simmer, covered, 10 minutes. Cool slightly. Purée in 2 batches in blender. Push purée through sieve to remove corn hulls and pepper skin. For ultimate smoothness, purée soup briefly one more time. Add cream if desired. Makes 4 ½ cups.

Soup Notes

SALAD DRESSINGS & SALADS

F rom day one, our green salad always meant cut soft lettuce with homemade vinaigrette dressing. Seasonal creativity kept our composed luncheon salads in perpetual evolution. Pasta salad reigned supreme.

Mary Jo's Vinaigrette

Everyone who worked in my kitchen made vinaigrette. We made thousands of gallons. This is the only dressing we ever used on our green salads, and this is the dressing we sold bottled. Plan to make the basic vinaigrette and the strong version at the same go, and keep them on hand in the refrigerator. Before you begin, mash 3–5 cloves of peeled, sliced garlic in a small mortar with ½ teaspoon of salt to form a paste.

1 teaspoon garlic paste
4 fl. oz. (½ cup) red wine vinegar
2 teaspoons Dijon mustard
¾ teaspoon salt
2 tablespoons white wine
10 fl. oz. (1¼ cups) olive oil or a mixture of olive oil and sunflower or canola oil

1. In a blender jar combine garlic, vinegar, mustard, salt, and wine. Whiz to blend thoroughly. Add oil and quickly pulse blender once or twice to mix oil and vinegar. (Any further blending will cause the dressing to thicken.) Pour into a pint jar, cover, and refrigerate until ready to use.

Remember that olive oil will solidify when chilled. Shake or stir well before using. Makes 2 cups.

STRONG VINAIGRETTE

Strong means this vinaigrette has more vinegar. We used this dressing as a base for all pasta, rice, chicken, and potato salads.

1 teaspoon garlic paste

6 fl. oz. (¾ cup) red wine vinegar

2 teaspoons Dijon mustard

¾ teaspoon salt

8 fl. oz. (I cup) sunflower oil or a combination of olive and vegetable oils

Prepare using the method on page 26. Makes almost 2 cups.

TOMATO VINAIGRETTE

Tomato paste gives color and flavor, making this a dressing for all seasons.

3 oz. (⅓ cup) tomato paste
1 tablespoon olive oil
¼ teaspoon ground allspice
¼ teaspoon turmeric
1 teaspoon paprika
⅛ teaspoon cayenne
2 cloves garlic
½ fresh green or red chili with seeds (optional)
½ teaspoon salt
1 tablespoon balsamic vinegar
8 fl. oz. (1 cup) Strong Vinaigrette (p. 27)

1. Heat 1 tablespoon oil in a no-stick frying pan. Add tomato paste and mash it about, stirring constantly to gently "cook" paste. Add allspice, turmeric, paprika, cayenne and continue to cook, stirring constantly for a few minutes or until spices smell fragrant. Cool.

2. Mash garlic and optional chili to purée with salt. When seasoned tomato paste has cooled, stir in garlic and balsamic vinegar. Gradually whisk in Strong Vinaigrette. Store dressing in glass jar in refrigerator. Plan to make dressing a day or several hours before using to allow flavors to blend and color to bloom. Makes about 1½ cups.

Note: You will need a generous cup of this dressing for 4 pounds mixed pasta, vegetables, and chicken to serve 6–8.

Lemon Vinaigrette For Asparagus Pasta Salad

When spring asparagus is abundant in the fields and plastic tubs of green spears stand in the fridge, this is a splendid luncheon dish. Toss lightly blanched asparagus, freshly cooked pasta, fresh tarragon, scallions—and a little pulled chicken if you wish—with this lemon sauce. Lavender chive flowers should be in the garden and would make a delicate garnish. This dressing also complements green beans, broccoli or cauliflower.

1 medium lemon, scrubbed, grated, and juiced
1 clove garlic mashed with salt
1 teaspoon Dijon mustard
1/8 teaspoon turmeric
3 or 4 thin slices green chili including seeds, minced (optional)
2 fl. oz. (4 tablespoons) heavy cream
4½ fl. oz. (9 tablespoons) Strong Vinaigrette (p. 27)
fresh or dry tarragon to taste

Into lemon juice and zest, mix crushed garlic, mustard, turmeric and chili. Stir in cream, Strong Vinaigrette, and tarragon to taste. Makes 1 cup.

LEMON CURRY VINAIGRETTE

A dazzling dressing for rice salads, grilled chicken, or vegetables. The dressing must be made several hours ahead for the best flavor, and it keeps well for days.

1½ teaspoons ground coriander

½ teaspoon ground cumin

½ teaspoon turmeric

⅛ teaspoon cayenne

2 teaspoons curry powder

2 tablespoons sunflower or other salad oil

zest and juice of 1 medium lemon (3 tablespoons juice)

½ serrano chili minced, seeds included (or other fresh chili to taste)

1 or 2 cloves garlic, mashed to a paste with ¼ teaspoon salt

½ teaspoon Dijon mustard

2 tablespoons diced preserved lemon rind (p. 119)

6 fl. oz. (¾ cup) Strong Vinaigrette (p. 27)

1. Heat a small heavy skillet over moderate flame. Combine ground coriander, cumin, turmeric, cayenne, and curry powder in small cup. When skillet is warm, add all ground spices to pan and stir over heat until fragrant, about 2 minutes; do not let spices burn. Scrape hot spice powder back into cup; mix in 2 tablespoons salad oil and allow to cool to lukewarm. (This step is optional, though the heating will bring out better flavor in the spices.)

2. In blender jar combine lemon zest, lemon juice, chili, mashed garlic, and mustard. Blend to thoroughly mince all ingredients. Add oil with spices and whiz to combine. Add diced preserved lemon, Strong Vinaigrette, and mix on low speed to chop lemon. Pour dressing into jam jar. Refrigerate dressing several hours or overnight to combine flavors before using. Makes 10 ounces.

EARL

"How's them chickens, Mary Jo?" was the usual response when I answered the phone most Tuesdays around ten. Earl was ready for my weekly poultry order, to be delivered the next day.

For as long as people in Hamilton, Ohio can remember, behind the twenty-foot white, red, and yellow grossly regal plastic chicken on Dixie Highway stood a low-slung, dilapidated building where you could buy fresh chicken, eggs, and a few Italian cheeses. Danny's Poultry delivered sizable orders to neighborhood homes, markets, and restaurants. Earl stopped at my house, supplying my cottage-industry catering business, and later at my shop where I needed whole chickens for stock, salads, curries, and stews; chicken breasts for dinners; plus occasional turkeys and ducks. My patrons claimed Earl's must have been some sort of religious chicken; it was that much better than the Amish variety sold in supermarkets!

Danny must have started his fresh poultry venture early in the nineteen-fifties when the birds were processed on the premises. Once in a while in the seventies I used to drive by. Although the stench was potent, the counters were clean, the chicken cold, and the product worth the trip. Danny worked hard, made good money, and owned a fleet of Cadillacs.

After he was discharged from the Army in Korea, Earl came to work for Danny. He was barely twenty-three, newly married to a teenage bride, and just up from the hill country to the bright city. Broken-toothed and scraggy, Earl plucked, cleaned, cut up, and packaged chickens. He ran the deliveries and paid his dues to the boss until the early nineties when he bought the business. Everything rolled along in a reliably ramshackle, backwoods sort of way that kept us all in chicken and Earl's kids off the streets.

Earl staffed his broken-down vans with rough guys clad in white plastic coats. They hauled in dripping boxes of chicken through icy winters and steaming summers. They tacked pink bills on my shop board and collected monthly payments.

The health department pressed in. Danny had passed away; his widow saw the rent checks stop. No one answered the phone at Danny's Poultry. It was rumored, Earl had gone south. He may have lost the business, and we all lost the chicken. I never had the moment to say goodbye to my chicken man of twenty-five years, and I never knew his last name.

Thai Peanut Dressing

Another favorite with pasta salads, exotically sweet, hot, tart, and salty.

5 oz. (½ cup) peanut butter

2 tablespoons Asian sesame oil

2 cloves garlic mashed to a paste with salt

1 teaspoon brown sugar (omit if peanut butter contains sugar)

½ to 1 teaspoon finely chopped fresh chili, including seeds, or ⅛
teaspoon cayenne

⅛ teaspoon turmeric

2–4 tablespoons soy sauce

juice ½ lemon or 1 lime

8 fl. oz. (1 cup) Strong Vinaigrette (p. 27)

1. Measure peanut butter into medium mixing bowl; stir in sesame oil, garlic, brown sugar, chili, turmeric, and soy sauce. Blend in lemon juice. Note that peanut butter may stiffen as liquid is added.

2. Gradually whisk in strong vinaigrette, as if making mayonnaise. If emulsion breaks and sauce looks curdled, add ½ tablespoon water and whisk until mixture is smooth. Taste for seasonings, adding more soy or lemon if needed. Makes 1¾ cups dressing.

This amount will dress a 4-pound mixture of pasta, vegetables, and chicken prepared for salad. The dressing may be stored in a jar in the refrigerator for 2 weeks. It also makes an excellent satay dip for grilled chicken or pork.

How To Make a Small Quantity Of Mayonnaise By Hand

The luxury of mayonnaise is often considered an anathema among today's fat-conscious diners. Although I would never consider dipping a spoon into a jar of bottled brand, the exquisite flavor of handmade mayonnaise should not be missed. The magic of its preparation is an exercise of almost spiritual delight. Have patience and a steady hand as you observe the transformation of an egg yolk and a little oil into a silken sauce.

1 egg yolk (organic or free range)

¼ teaspoon Dijon mustard

1–2 teaspoons lemon juice or white wine vinegar

4 fl. oz. (½ cup) oil (2 tablespoons olive oil plus 6 tablespoons sunflower
    or canola oil)

pinch of salt

1. Place a 1-quart glass bowl on damp cloth on flat surface. (The cloth holds the bowl steady.) Using a small stainless whisk, break up egg yolk with mustard and 1 teaspoon lemon juice.

2. Place oil in measuring cup with pouring lip or in small creamer. If you are right-handed, hold oil cup in your left hand and keep whisk in your right hand. As you consistently turn egg yolk in circles with whisk, pour in oil a few drops at a time. As soon as the emulsion begins to form and the oil is absorbed into the yolk, you may increase oil flow to a thin stream. Continue to whisk and pour in oil until stiff golden sauce forms. Season with pinch of salt and add a little more lemon juice if desired. Makes ½ cup. Homemade mayonnaise will keep well for 1 week in refrigerator.

Note: If the mayonnaise "breaks" or the oil separates from the egg, it needs a simple remedy: Leave 1 tablespoon of the broken sauce in the bowl and pour the remainder into the measuring cup. Add ¼ teaspoon Dijon mustard to the bowl and whisk together. Very gradually, a few drops at a time at first, add the broken sauce to the bowl as you "remount" the emulsion.

Equipment

The Bread Mixer —

My old horse of a Hobart came on the sly. In early catering days, with fifty dollars in my pocket, I met a restaurant equipment dealer, in a Cincinnati parking lot, who heaved the heavy machine from his car trunk into my family station wagon.

The twelve-quart mixer was rough and repainted. Its bowl was thinning with rust, yet it kneaded tons of yeast dough, whisked clouds of meringue, and paddle-creamed barrels of butter. Drops of mineral oil kept the hoist free as the motor purred over the years.

The Grinding Stone —

My children argue over who will get my grinding stone. I purchased the hand-chiseled, black lava-rock bowl in Dar es Salaam in 1964. The ten-pound stone weighted pâtés, held doors open, and was the perfect mortar. The nineteen-inch dark mahogany pestle, dented with softened nicks from Sayidi's whacks at an African propane cylinder cap, came as a gift from the Sikh postmaster's wife in the remote village of Songea, Tanzania. From pestos to salsas and green masalas, no electric device provided the even, hand-wrought smoothness of the stone.

A palm-high, four-pound brass mortar, with its hand-length solid pestle of Indian origin, crushed peppercorns or coriander seeds. The wooden mortar, a modest square with a hollow center, was wedded to a small Syrian wooden pounder, a treasure from Accra in Ghana. Garlic for all our vinaigrettes began the journey in this bowl.

The Cookware —
Black skillets from Depression-era Colorado, well-seasoned from bacon grease and venison steak frys, hung from hooks beside the range along with French steel crepe and omelet pans. Long ago I'd learned to scour these pans with salt over heat and to keep them in use to prevent rust. These cured old bits of scrap were heirlooms.

Blue enameled braising pans, slick with burned-on black, could not be replaced. A shelf full of heavy iron Le Creuset may have been chipped and scarred, but they were top notch for long simmers.

No one touched my knives. The restaurant kitchen wall magnet was divided between knives for me and knives for thee, and the blades never crossed.

Electric blenders and processors came and went, but nothing topped the Robot Coup and the Osterizer, and three KitchenAids lined the pastry counter.

Salads

About Pasta Salads —

O.K., here's my secret: I bought my house on pasta salad. This method produces the best pasta salads, and this product was my main money-maker. Everyone likes spaghetti; noodle salads make great lunch, picnic, or buffet items. We added lots of vegetables, poached chicken, or cheeses, sometimes lentils, always bits of sweet roasted carrot, and used an array of delicious dressings that kept our customers coming back for more.

Here are a few guidelines:

All of our pasta salad dressings are based on the Strong Vinaigrette recipe. Tomato Vinaigrette, Lemon Curry, Thai Peanut, and Lemon Cream are included in this chapter. However, your imagination can take you anywhere with pasta salad dressings. Consider: Honey-Mustard, Caesar, Ginger-Soy, Pesto, or Aztec with puréed ancho peppers and cumin.

One pound of dry pasta will make enough salad for 14–16 servings. Calculate 1 oz. dry pasta per serving. One pound of dry pasta will cook up to nearly $2^1/2$ pounds, drained weight. Pasta must be cooked shortly before putting the salad together. Cold, refrigerated pasta has a pasty flavor. For pasta salad served on the plate, my noodle of preference is linguine. For pasta in takeout dishes where guests will be serving themselves, larger noodles such as bow ties are more manageable.

Plan 2 oz. skinless, boneless poached chicken per serving. Chicken may be cooked ahead, pulled, and refrigerated. One medium chicken will make enough to serve 8–10 in pasta salad. Leftover roast pork or beef, when thinly sliced and cut in ribbons, or flaked grilled fish, may be added in place of chicken.

Roasted carrots may be made ahead and will keep up to a week, tightly covered in the fridge. They add a special texture, bright color, and a touch of sweetness.

Prepare at least 2 blanched green vegetables for each salad, and plan 3 oz. cut vegetables per serving. Include a generous addition of finely chopped green onions, fresh parsley, and when in season, add mint, dill, or basil. In winter when green vegetables may be lacking, the occasional handful of shredded Napa cabbage or broken fresh spinach will fluff out a pasta salad. French or brown lentils are welcome additions.

Chicken may be prepared a day ahead. Blanched vegetables are best if not refrigerated after cooking, but will stand at room temperature for a couple of hours. Pasta should be cooked as close to serving time as possible. However, do, of course, refrigerate all leftovers; they will be good the next day, but not as bright as when freshly mixed, because vinegar will dull green vegetables.

I think you now get the picture of how, for very little money and a little ingenuity, you can produce main dish salads that will amaze and please every palate.

GREEN VEGETABLES FOR PASTA SALAD

Choose seasonably appropriate vegetables whenever possible. Save the broccoli, cauliflower, Brussels sprouts for winter; use asparagus, green beans, sugar snaps, zucchini, and delicate greens for spring and summer.

Plan to cook the vegetables in boiling salted water before cooking the pasta. (Saves on energy and cleanup!) Cut broccoli to separate the crown from the stem. Cut cauliflower in quarters. Snap off tough ends from asparagus. Remove only the stem end from green beans. Leave zucchini whole and remove tough ribs from kale or chard.

Bring a large pot of water to a boil; add 2 tablespoons of salt for 4 quarts of water. (Water should taste salty and salt will maintain vegetable color.) Cook each vegetable separately and do not crowd the pan. Add only enough so that the boil is maintained or very quickly returns. Time should be calculated with water boiling and uncovered. Each vegetable should be cooked until it is crisply tender. Plan 2 minutes for broccoli crowns and cauliflower; 4 minutes for broccoli stems. Green beans need 4 minutes; sugar snaps only 1 minute, snow peas just seconds; give small to medium zucchini 2 minutes and greens only time to wilt and tenderize. As you lift each vegetable from the boiling water with a slotted spoon or a Chinese spider (a wire mesh scoop with a wooden handle), spread the veggies out on baking sheets to cool.

Note: Many cooks "shock" blanched vegetables by immersing them in ice water. I do not recommend this process, for it removes flavor, makes them waterlogged, and creates excess hassle. Slightly undercooking the vegetables and allowing them to cool in lots of space works fine.

When the vegetables have cooled to room temperature, cut them into desired shapes and sizes for salads: Cut broccoli and cauliflower into small florets; peel broccoli stems and slice into coins or sticks. Diagonally cut green beans into halves or thirds. Cut zucchini in half lengthwise and then chop into narrow diagonal slices. Diagonally halve snow peas or sugar snaps. Diagonally cut asparagus into bite-sized pieces. Roll greens and cut into ribbons.

IRREVERENT METHOD OF COOKING PASTA

Some cooks are offended by this method; however, it works perfectly, takes less energy, and avoids extra kitchen heat in summer. This is easiest with a gas range. On an electric stove, the cooking pot will have to be removed from the burner when the heat is turned off.

Bring a large pot of water to a boil and throw in a handful of salt—or preferably cook pasta in the already salted water after blanching salad vegetables. Add the pasta (break long noodles in half for easier eating in a salad unless custom-bound to whole pasta), stir well, and return to the boil for 2 minutes. Stir again; turn off heat; cover and allow to stand 7 minutes for linguine or 9–10 minutes for larger shapes. Taste for al dente doneness, and pour off into a colander. Rinse pasta with cold water to stop cooking.

Shake off excess water, turn pasta into bowl, and coat with 1 tablespoon olive oil per pound of pasta.

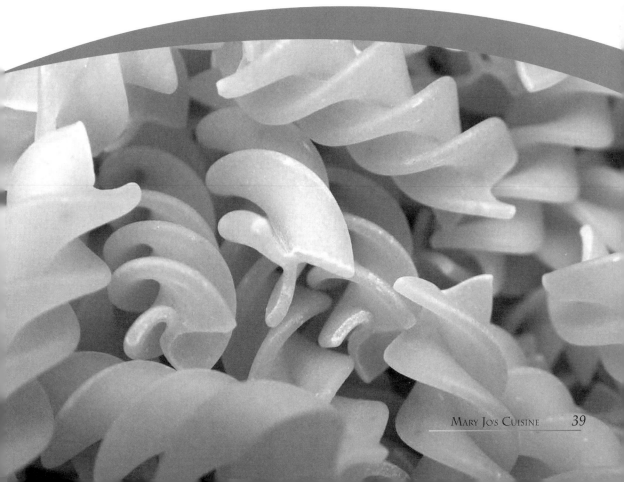

ROASTED CARROTS FOR PASTA SALAD

One pound raw carrots will give 4–5 ounces roasted carrots, enough for a salad serving 8–10. These carrots will keep refrigerated for a week and can be frozen. Children enjoy eating them like candy. Whenever you have the oven on at length, roast a tray of carrots; you'll find all sorts of uses for these gems. If a few on the edges get too dark, save them for stock or a stew when you want a rich brown color.

Top and tail the carrots, peel, and diagonally slice into ¼-inch thick ovals. Lightly coat with olive oil (2 teaspoons per pound). Strew carrots on baking sheet, making sure they do not overlap; sprinkle with salt. Roast in 350°F oven 45–50 minutes. You may stir carrots halfway through cooking. They are done when shriveled, brightly colored, and tender. Cool and refrigerate in covered container.

POACHED CHICKEN FOR SALADS

Poaching chicken on the stovetop is easy to control and gives the benefit of luxurious stock for soups and sauces. Chicken for salads may also be roasted or grilled, though poaching gives the most delicate, moist meat. I always advise poaching a whole chicken; chicken parts easily overcook.

1 3½–4 lb. whole chicken
1 medium onion, sliced
1 carrot, sliced
1 rib celery, sliced
2 cloves garlic
1 bay leaf
parsley sprigs
thyme sprigs or pinch of dry thyme
½ teaspoon peppercorns
1 teaspoon salt

1. Choose saucepan that will hold chicken snugly when placed on its back in bottom of pan. Surround chicken with vegetables and seasonings. Add water until chicken is almost submerged. Cover saucepan; bring to boil. Reduce heat and simmer for 45–50 minutes or until chicken tests done. To test chicken for doneness, remove from broth; pull down leg/thigh joint and check to see if juices run clear and if meat is no longer reddish pink. Breast meat will cook faster than leg meat. If you test chicken breast with an instant-read thermometer and it registers 145°F, yet the thigh portion still shows a bit of pink, break off leg/thigh portions of chicken and return them to hot, turned-off broth and allow them to stand covered for 10 more minutes. The thigh will register 160°F when cooked through.

2. Allow cooked chicken to rest until cool enough to handle. Remove skin and lift meat from bones in large chunks. Return skin and bones to stock and continue to simmer for another hour or 2 before straining broth. When chicken meat is cool enough to handle, pull meat into bite-sized chunks, removing any bits of gristle or tendon. Cool cooked chicken to room temperature. Cover and chill or mix into a salad. A 4-pound chicken will normally yield 1¼ pounds of lean pulled chicken for salad. Save broth for soups or sauces. (See Chicken Stock for Soups) (p. 3)

CHICKEN PASTA SALAD

This is a basic formula for a luncheon or supper salad to serve four. You will find the mixture changes with the vegetables and herbs in season. Other meats or fish may be substituted for the chicken; lentils or black beans may be included for a vegetarian salad. These amounts will provide a 2¼-pound mixture before the dressing is added. Serves 4.

4 oz. dry linguine, or other pasta
8 oz. (2 cups) poached, pulled chicken (p. 41)
1 lb. (4 cups) blanched, cut green vegetables
1–2 oz. (¼–½ cup) roasted carrots
4–5 green onions, thinly sliced
generous ½ cup Tomato or other seasoned vinaigrette (p. 28–32)
fresh parsley, basil, dill, tarragon, cilantro or mint to taste

1. Cook vegetables and pasta according to directions under About Pasta Salads (p. 36–40); cool to room temperature.

2. In large bowl, combine chicken, pasta, vegetables, green onions, and toss with vinaigrette. Check for seasonings, adding more salt, a few drops of lemon, or vinegar if necessary. (For some reason large quantities of pasta salad always need more vinegar to lift the flavor.) Garnish with chopped fresh parsley and seasonal herbs. Serve as soon as possible after mixing in dressing.

Note: When using Tomato Vinaigrette, a garnish of crumbled feta cheese and a few Kalamata olives make lively additions.

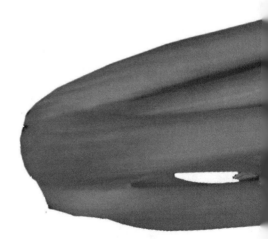

New London Chicken Salad

Long before I opened Mary Jo's, I prepared fifty pounds of this salad for the New London Ladies' Swim Club. It became a cafe luncheon standby for years until we needed to transport a quantity to a summer wedding. We replaced the mayonnaise with a creamy vinaigrette and used pickled ginger instead of candied ginger, giving a lighter rendition and one more suitable for a warm afternoon. The original dressing is also noted. Whatever form of ginger you use, do not use uncooked fresh ginger—a natural enzyme in fresh ginger will dissolve the chicken.

1 pound (4 cups) poached, pulled chicken (p. 41)
1 large tart apple, peeled and diced (8 oz. or 1½ cups)
⅔ cup finely chopped green onion
1 cup celery cut in small dice
salt and freshly ground pepper and fresh lemon juice to taste
roasted pecans or almonds, and grapes or melon for garnish

Dressing

1 clove garlic mashed with ½ teaspoon salt

2 tablespoons fresh lemon juice

2 teaspoons Dijon or grainy mustard or a mixture of both

4 tablespoons heavy cream

2 tablespoons olive oil

4 tablespoons vegetable oil (sunflower suggested)

1 tablespoon finely chopped fresh tarragon or 1 teaspoon dry tarragon

2 tablespoons slivered pickled ginger* or chopped candied ginger

lemon juice and Vinaigrette Dressing to taste (p. 26)

1. To make dressing, dissolve garlic and mustard in lemon juice. Whisk in cream, then oil. Stir in tarragon and ginger.

2. To make salad, combine chicken, apple, green onion, and celery in large mixing bowl. Fold in creamy vinaigrette and correct seasoning with salt, pepper, and lemon juice to taste.

3. Serve chicken salad on bed of soft salad greens lightly dressed with vinaigrette; garnish with roasted nuts, grapes, or melon and fresh parsley. Makes 2 pounds chicken salad; serves 5–6.

Note: For original dressing, combine ½ cup homemade mayonnaise (p. 33) with ¼ cup sour cream. Season with 1 teaspoon grainy mustard, fresh or dry tarragon, and 1 or 2 tablespoons chopped candied ginger.

Pickled Ginger

1 oz. (¼ cup packed) very thinly sliced peeled fresh ginger

2 tablespoons rice or cider vinegar

1 tablespoon water

1½ teaspoons sugar

pinch of salt

Place vinegar, water, sugar, and salt in small saucepan; bring to boil. Add ginger; return to boil. Remove from heat and cool. Makes 2 tablespoons drained pickled ginger.

Note: This is a good method to preserve ginger for salads when you have extra. Increase ingredients proportionally to ginger. Store in jam jar in fridge. Pickled ginger will keep 2 months.

BROWN RICE SALAD

We used rice salads for catered buffet meals and alternatives to pasta salad for luncheon. They can be made well ahead, are easy to serve and can be eaten with only a fork. The variations are limitless, with different rices and vegetable combinations plus assorted dressings. Here's an example:

7 oz. brown rice (1 cup)
1 tablespoon rice, red wine or cider vinegar
3 oz. Puy or brown lentils (½ cup)
1 bunch green onions, chopped (1½ cups)
2 oz. roasted carrots (½ cup)
1½ lbs. blanched cut green vegetables (6 cups)
4 oz. frozen baby peas (1 cup)
finely chopped parsley, mint, or cilantro
1 cup Lemon Curry Vinaigrette (p. 30) or another dressing

1. Rinse rice in cold water and drain thoroughly. Place in saucepan with tight fitting lid. Add 16 fl. oz. (2 cups) water, pinch of salt, stir, cover, and bring to a boil. Reduce heat to low and cook slowly about 40 minutes or until water is absorbed and rice is tender. While rice is still hot, sprinkle with vinegar; fluff with fork; cover with tea towel and allow to cool to lukewarm.

2. Cook lentils without salt in 1½ cups water for 12–15 minutes or until tender, but not mushy. Add salt; cool to room temperature; drain.

3. Prepare carrots and green vegetables as directed in About Pasta Salads (p. 36–40).

4. Combine all ingredients and dress with vinaigrette to taste; check for salt; garnish with seasonal herbs to taste. Serves 8 as a side dish.

Note: Add pulled poached chicken and a little extra dressing to make Chicken Rice Salad.

When making rice salad in quantity, consider mixing jasmine, brown, and wild rice for different colors and textures.

LENTIL SALAD

Lentil salads make steady buffet items, combine well with pasta or rice salads, and hold in the refrigerator for several days.

> 7 oz. (1 cup) French Puy lentils or regular brown lentils
> 24 fl. oz. (3 cups) water
> 1 teaspoon salt
> 4–6 tablespoons Strong Vinaigrette (p. 27)
> ½ cup chopped green onion
> 1 tablespoon chopped fresh dill or parsley
> finely chopped chili or freshly ground pepper to taste

1. Cover lentils with water, bring to boil, and simmer covered 12–15 minutes, or until tender but not mushy. Add salt and remove from heat. Allow to stand with salt for 5 minutes.

2. Drain lentils, shaking off cooking liquid. Place in bowl and add vinaigrette and chopped onion. Allow to stand 15 minutes to absorb seasoning. Add fresh herbs, chili, or pepper and more salt if necessary. Makes 2½ cups of salad.

Note: It is important to get the dressing on the lentils while they are still hot for the flavor to be absorbed. Feel free to add mint, cilantro, basil, or chervil in season. The salad may be extended with diced tomato, sweet peppers, cucumber, or sliced, blanched green beans. A generous sprinkling of crumbled feta and a few olives make the lentil salad a full meal.

French Potato Salad

This is the simplest and, for me, the finest potato salad. For the best flavor, the salad must be freshly made and kept out of the refrigerator. Choose small red, yellow, or white potatoes.

1 lb. small potatoes
3–4 green onions, thinly sliced
5–6 tablespoons Strong Vinaigrette (p. 27)
finely chopped fresh parsley, dill, tarragon, or chiffonade of basil
freshly ground black pepper

    Boil potatoes in salted water until tender. Pour off water; return saucepan to low heat and steam for 3–5 minutes. Uncover and, as soon as potatoes can be handled with a tea towel, lift from pan and cut into slices. (To peel or not to peel is your decision.) Layer sliced warm potatoes with chopped green onion and toss gently with vinaigrette. Potatoes must be dressed while warm for dressing to be absorbed. Season to taste with salt, pepper, adding chopped fresh herbs in season. Potato salad may be held at room temperature up to 4 hours. Serves 3.

CUCUMBER RAITA

We always included this raita with our curries. The cooling cucumber and yogurt duo plays a major role from Greece to eastern India.

1 cucumber (at least 10–12 oz.) or ½ large seedless cucumber
½ teaspoon salt
1 cup plain whole milk yogurt, preferably homemade (p. 21)
1 clove garlic mashed with a little salt
2 tablespoons chopped green onion
2 tablespoons chopped cilantro or fresh mint, dill, and parsley
½ teaspoon finely chopped green chili, seeds intact (optional)
salt and pepper to taste
sprinkle of ground cumin
diced fresh tomato in season (optional)

1. Peel cucumber, scrape out seeds with teaspoon. (Leave center intact if using seedless cucumber.) Cut into small dice. Place diced cucumber in a bowl; toss with salt and allow to stand 20–30 minutes. Rinse lightly; shake dry in a sieve; then place drained cucumber in a tea towel and twist to squeeze out most of water. Squeezed cucumber will be crisp, transparent, and half its original volume.

2. Mix garlic, onion, herbs, and optional chili into yogurt. Fold in cucumber. Season to taste with salt and pepper. Place in serving bowl and dust top with ground cumin. Garnish with more cilantro and optional tomato.

Panzanella: Italian Tomato And Bread Salad

In tomato season, there's nothing better than crusty bread sopped with sun-ripe tomatoes, a few herbs, and a drizzle of good olive oil. In early September, Panzanella would be the star attraction on our Mediterranean salad plate.

6 oz. (4 cups) large cubes of French or sourdough bread
2 lbs. ripe, juicy, homegrown tomatoes
1–2 cloves garlic mashed to a paste with ½ teaspoon salt
1 small anchovy fillet (optional)
¼ teaspoon chopped fresh green or red chili with seeds (optional)
2 tablespoons red wine vinegar
5–6 tablespoons fruity olive oil
¼ cup chopped sweet onion or green onions
handful of torn fresh basil or chopped parsley
salt and pepper to taste
2 teaspoons balsamic vinegar (optional)

1. Toast bread cubes lightly, in moderate oven, until crisp and golden on edges, but not hard all the way through.

2. Scald tomatoes 10 seconds. Core, peel, cut in half at equator, and gently squeeze each half into sieve placed over bowl. Rub tomato seeds with back of ladle to extract juice. Discard seeds; save juice and cut tomatoes into medium chunks. The result should yield 4 cups tomato chunks and 1 cup tomato juice.

3. In bottom of large bowl, mash garlic with optional anchovy and finely chopped chili. Whisk in vinegar and olive oil. Add tomatoes, juice, bread cubes, and onion. Allow mixture to stand an hour for bread to absorb juices.

4. Before serving, mix in fresh basil and/or parsley. Taste for seasonings, adding more salt and pepper or perhaps a dash of balsamic vinegar if needed. For extravagance, drizzle top with another spoonful of olive oil. Serves 4.

Note: This salad may be further embellished with peeled roasted red or yellow pepper strips, cucumber slices, black Greek olives, whole anchovy fillets, or shaved Parmesan.

Sweet Potato Salad

This salad came into my files one November when I needed a sweet potato dish for a Thanksgiving-inspired cold buffet. We featured it on our Thanksgiving salad plate and our Thanksgiving takeout dinner. I've never looked back to a sweet potato casserole. This salad can easily be made 1–2 days ahead.

3 medium sweet potatoes* (1¼ lbs.)

3 tablespoons finely chopped green onions

1 medium carrot (4 oz.)

4–5 tablespoons Strong Vinaigrette (p. 27)

½ tablespoon lemon juice

2 teaspoons grated fresh ginger (use microplane or very small holes on grater)

chopped fresh parsley or cilantro

* Choose sweet potatoes with dark skin and deep orange flesh. They are reliably good from late summer through December. Raw sweet potatoes must not be stored under refrigeration or they become bland and mealy.

1. Place sweet potatoes on small baking tray and roast in 350°F–400°F oven until very soft.

2. Meanwhile, chop onion; peel and cut carrot into ⅛-inch dice. Steam or blanch carrot briefly to intensify color. Carrot should retain a bite. Mix vinaigrette with lemon juice and ginger.

3. As soon as baked sweet potatoes can be handled (be sure to work with them while they are still very warm), peel and cut them into large dice. Many of them will break apart, but that is O.K.

4. Fold onion, carrot, and vinaigrette mixture into sweet potatoes. Season with salt and pepper; garnish with parsley. Makes a generous pound and will serve 4.

CRANBERRY RELISH

We sold buckets of this relish for carryout every November. Caramelized sugar, a few spices, and a touch of chili give this cranberry sauce a lift.

½ orange, 2 oz. (½ cup diced)
½ lemon, 2 oz. (½ cup diced)
1 tablespoon grated fresh ginger
1 cinnamon stick
⅛–¼ teaspoon crushed red pepper
5 oz. sugar (⅔ cup plus 1 tablespoon)
4 fl. oz. (½ cup) apple cider or water
12 oz. bag cranberries, fresh or frozen
1½ oz. currants (¼ cup) (optional)

1. Cut orange and lemon into thin slices, then into small dice, removing seeds.

2. Melt sugar with pinch of salt and cinnamon stick in heavy saucepan or stainless steel skillet. As soon as melted sugar becomes light amber, add diced lemon, orange, cider or water, ginger, and red pepper. Cover and cook gently 15 minutes. Sugar will dissolve and cook into syrup.

3. Remove cover; add cranberries and ¼ cup water. Stir well and cook until cranberries pop; about 5 minutes. Add currants and more liquid if sauce seems too thick. Cool, pour into glass jar, and refrigerate. Makes 3 cups. Cranberry relish may be stored in refrigerator for a month or may be frozen.

Salad Notes

QUICHE

For years I was the luncheon Queen of Quiche. Quiche made great party food. Ellen wanted quiche for company. Alice stopped for supper slices. Everybody asked for quiche to the point that sometimes I'd make unusual fillings, like buttered cabbage and blue cheese or layered purée of carrot and Swiss chard, so I could sell something else. With perfect pastry and rich custard, the range of possible fillings was endless.

We managed the daily quiche program by spending part of one afternoon each week organizing the prep. We refrigerated logs of pastry, plastic boxes of grated cheese, gallons of filling, and bowls of sautéed onions with garlic.

A food processor is a bonus here. If the pastry is made first, the cheese grated second, and the filling mixed third, the processor bowl needs to be washed only once at the end. Each evening I rolled the shells for the next day and placed them in the refrigerated case. The following morning I rounded up the veg and layered in the filling.

QUICHE PASTRY
PIE CRUST
PÂTE BRISÉE

Makes 30 oz. of pastry, enough for three 9-by-1½-inch quiche shells.
A quiche pan is a deep tart pan with a removable bottom.

1 lb. (3½ cups) all-purpose flour
1 ¼ teaspoon salt (1 teaspoon if using salted butter)
9 oz. cold butter (2 ¼ sticks) or 8 oz. butter plus
1 oz. lard* (2 tablespoons)
5 fl. oz. (10 tablespoons) ice water

Note: For delicate pastry use 14 oz. all-purpose flour plus 2 oz. cake flour to approximate pastry flour. Nice to try if you have cake flour on hand.

1. a) To make pastry by hand: Sift flour and salt into mound on cool, flat surface (clean counter top is fine), or into wide bowl. Slice over butter and lard; "cut" it into flour using dough scraper, pastry blender or dull knife, until butter is size of large peas. Use your fingertips to press butter into floured flakes, making sure there is a layer of flour between warm fingers and cold butter. Spread flour and butter meal into circle and sprinkle with ice water. Quickly bring dough together by drawing your fingers inward through meal to form integrated ball. Scrape pastry bits from counter into dough ball. Push dough out with heel of your hand and pull it together once more to distribute moisture. Scrape any dough bits off your hands and add to pastry. Shape dough into 6-inch log, wrap, and refrigerate.

b) To make pastry in food processor: Place flour and salt in work bowl. Add cold butter and lard cut; in ½-inch cubes or slices. Pulse 3 times to break butter into flakes. With processor running, pour ice water in slow stream through feed tube. Stop processor as soon as pastry rolls into ball. Remove ball of dough from bowl; shape into 6-inch log. Wrap in plastic and refrigerate.

2. To roll a shell: Shape 10 oz. chilled pastry (one-third of batch) into 4-inch disk. Dust with flour and roll on smooth, clean surface, giving dough a quarter turn with each rolling to maintain circle. Roll to generous 12-inch circle; brush off excess flour. Fold in quarters; unfold inside quiche pan. Press pastry firmly into bottom edge of pan. Use scissors to trim dough to an even ¼-inch overhang. Tuck overhang inside pastry edge, pressing firmly. Crimp or flute top edge. Chill pastry shell at least ½ hour before baking. Chilling relaxes gluten in flour, prevents shrinkage, and cracking. In haste, shell may be chilled in freezer 10 minutes. (If you plan to make 1 quiche at a time, press leftover bits of pastry onto remaining log; wrap and freeze.)

* The addition of lard always makes the tenderest pastry; however, lard must be purchased from a reliable butcher. Freeze lard for storage.

Quiche Filling

This recipe makes enough filling for 2 quiches. Make the full amount and freeze half for a second quiche, or divide the recipe in half, using 3 eggs for 1 quiche. Use a food processor or a blender to mix the filling. The idea for this filling stems from Elizabeth David's Quiche au Fromage Blanc.

8 oz. cream cheese, room temperature

8 fl. oz. (1 cup) whole milk

8 fl. oz. (1 cup) heavy cream (or substitute 2 cups half-and-half for milk and cream)

5 eggs (large or extra-large)

¾ teaspoon salt

freshly ground white pepper

generous grating fresh nutmeg

pinch cayenne (optional)

Cut cream cheese into 1-inch chunks and place around processor bowl or in blender jar. Add milk and process. Scrape down sides and mix to a smooth, dense cream. Add eggs, salt, pepper, nutmeg, cayenne, and cream or remaining half-and-half to processor or blender. Whiz to combine. Use straightaway or refrigerate in plastic container. Makes generous quart.

QUICHE BASICS

Quiche onion and garlic:

For each 9-inch quiche you will need ²/₃ cup sautéed onion and garlic. To prepare, finely chop 2 cloves garlic for each large onion (10–12 oz.) cut in small dice. Melt a tablespoon of butter or a mixture of butter and olive oil in a deep sauté pan. First add diced onion; place chopped garlic on top. Cover with butter papers and cook over low heat until the onion is totally limp, soft, and not browned. Season with salt and stir together. 1½ cups diced raw onion will yield ²/₃ cup cooked onion. Prepare as much as you need for quiche or make extra to perk up leftovers or omelets.

Quiche cheese:

For each 9-inch quiche, you will need 6 oz. grated cheese. I recommend a mixture of aged white Cheddar and nutty-flavored Swiss cheese. You may choose Jarlsberg, Gruyère, Emmentaler, Wisconsin, Vermont, imported Cheddar, or any number of firm white cheeses. A mixture of cheeses always makes quiche more interesting, but a distinctive Cheddar or Swiss may be used alone.

Baking beans:

Keep a tin of dry beans (navy, pinto, black, or great northern) to weight down pastry shells when baking "blind" or half-baking before adding a filling. This process is the only way to ensure a crisp bottom crust. The baking beans and the lining foil may be used over and over; the beans will last for years. When the hulls shrivel and loosen, sift or winnow them away from the beans.

QUICHE BAKING PROCEDURE

1. Preheat oven to 400°F. Line chilled pastry with 12-inch square sheet of foil. Carefully press foil into lower edge of shell. Pour ½ inch baking beans into foil and bake 20–25 minutes. Pastry edges should begin to brown, and crust under foil should have lost "raw" look. Remove foil and beans. Pour beans back into tin, fold foil sheet, and store for next quiche or tart shell.

2. Immediately layer in filling. A hot pan and hot pastry encourage faster cooking and lessen chance of shell cracking. Into warm pastry shell, sprinkle all but 2 tablespoons of grated cheese. Spread cooked onion with garlic over cheese. Evenly distribute seasoned vegetable mixture of choice on top of onion. Finish with finely chopped parsley, dill, or basil and last bit of grated cheese. Carefully ladle over quiche filling, taking care not to reach top of shell. (If you cannot get all the filling in, pour the remaining bit in a small cup. Place the quiche in hot oven. Reach in and empty cup over quiche; again do not allow filling to spill over the edge.)

3. Bake filled quiche 25–40 minutes or until puffed and golden. Cool briefly on wire rack before serving. Makes 6 generous slices.

Note: Quiche is most flavorful at room temperature.

Reheating Quiche

Quiche is best the day it is baked. If it must be baked a day ahead, store in a cool room rather than fridge. Before serving, place quiche in pan or on baking sheet in 325°F oven for 20 minutes, until pastry crisps and filling warms. If quiche must be frozen, defrost, uncovered, overnight in fridge before heating. If necessary, slices of quiche may be taken directly from freezer to oven.

SÍLVIA

For a while we had Sílvia. Slender, Castilian-fair, with a black braid, she had come to Ohio as the young bride of the wild brother in the local taquería. She spoke no English and was spending days alone in a tiny bedroom, until my Spanish-fluent friend heard her story and encouraged her to venture into our kitchen. Here she was among women and close to familiar household chores.

She peeled onions without tears, scrubbed pots until they shone, and got down on hands and knees to clean corners. She taught me the Spanish names for produce and utensils – zanahoria was carrot, cuchara was spoon – and was delighted with the take-home pay. I knew she was undocumented, but I was so grateful for the good help – aware of how few American university students would work as hard as she – that I didn't care. When Sílvia became pregnant, she took time off for the baby's birth. Weeks later she came trundling back with Elizabeth in a stroller. I bought a playpen, put it in a protected corner, and we watched the child sleep and passed her around when she woke. We gave her crusts of bread when she was teething and fed her soft bits of chicken or potato. For months Lizzie was part of our family, and Sílvia was happy among her new aunties.

One day at the peak of lunch hour, the health inspector marched in, brandishing her thermometers right and left, thrusting one into a puffed, steaming quiche straight out of the oven, and another into a pristine chicken salad nestled in a deep bowl of ice. She trooped to the back and found our baby quiet in her playpen, tapping a metal bowl with a wooden spoon. She scolded me, saying the kitchen was no place for a child no matter how careful we were, no matter that those of us working were mothers as well.

We tried moving Elizabeth and the playpen into the back hall, but she cried. We tried putting her in the dining room during the day, but she cried. We all stood in fear of the health inspector, and one day Sílvia told us she was afraid to return to work. She packed up and left for Chicago.

ASPARAGUS QUICHE

Divine when asparagus is spring-fresh.

1 9-inch unbaked quiche shell, chilled (p. 56)
1¼ lb. tender, fresh asparagus (buy extra if ends are tough)
⅔ cup quiche onion and garlic (p. 59)
16 fl. oz. (2 cups) quiche filling (p. 58)
6 oz. (1½ cups) quiche cheese (p. 59)
finely chopped parsley, dill, or tarragon

1. Diagonally slice asparagus into 1-inch pieces. Cook cut asparagus quickly in ½ cup boiling, salted water until tender. Drain. Allow 2½–3 cups sliced cooked asparagus for each quiche.

2. Follow Quiche Baking Procedure (p. 60)

Broccoli And Sweet Pepper Quiche

Blanched broccoli prepared for salad or left from dinner is ready for quiche. Colorful sautéed pepper brightens the top.

1 9-inch unbaked quiche shell, chilled (p. 56)

1 bunch broccoli

1 yellow or red pepper diced, sautéed in olive oil, and seasoned

2/3 cup quiche onion and garlic (p. 59)

16 fl. oz. (2 cups) quiche filling (p. 58)

6 oz. (1½ cups) quiche cheese (p. 59)

finely chopped parsley or dill

1. To prepare broccoli, follow directions under How to Cook Green Vegetables (p. 151).

2. For an attractive pattern, wheel florets around outer circle of quiche on top of cheese and onions. Distribute peeled stem slices over center; top with sautéed pepper. Follow Quiche Baking Procedure (p. 60).

The Formula

Thirty-some years before I put out my shingle, my aunt Margie took me to dinner at The Copper Kettle in Aspen, Colorado. Even as a teenager, I was charmed by the set-menu concept of dining. I didn't have to worry about ordering too much or choosing something too expensive. It was perfect dining freedom.

When Mary Jo's Cuisine began serving dinner, I decided to present what we now call a prix-fixe menu. No one else in my area was offering a set menu. It became a niche; Mary Jo's became a destination. With one person managing the cooking and presenting the dinner, it worked.

Early on I settled on soups alone for the first course because they could be made ahead, were easy to heat, and get to the table fast. We made exceptional soups with homemade stocks and fresh vegetables in an age when good soup was hard to find. On a busy night when guests were quickly served crusty bread and a puréed soup, they were content, even if they had to wait longer for the main course. Our minimal costs for homemade soup and bread came back in waves of good will from our patrons.

Our salad was always the same: a plate of freshly washed and cut soft lettuce dressed with our French vinaigrette. We added garnishes of fresh tomato in summer, pomegranate seeds in winter. Our main course options included a chicken dish — most of the time a stuffed chicken breast; a meat that was often a braise or a roast; and a cooked-to-order fish, usually salmon filet with a classic sauce. We provided vegetarian meals on request. Colorful, seasonal fresh vegetables enhanced every plate. Four desserts were on order each evening: our signature bread pudding with custard sauce, a chocolate torte, a fruit pie or tart, and one of the great American cakes served with homemade ice cream.

With a fixed-price menu, there was the guarantee that each filled seat would bring in the tab for a whole dinner. We soon learned not to split a dinner between two — except for children of good patrons.

We also learned that, with our bare-bones staff, we couldn't fill our dining room twice in an evening. Inevitably the people who booked early arrived late, and those booking late arrived early. We didn't have space for a waiting area; we didn't want to rush the service; and to keep the tension down, we let guests know the table was theirs for the evening. Controlled seating also played into the waitress's benefit when we added an automatic gratuity. The secure tip money kept service even and gracious. Our ideal team, when we served thirty-five covers on a weekend evening, was to have one expert waitress who fully understood the menu, myself at the stove, and a speedy student on wash-up.

HAM AND MUSHROOM QUICHE

Ham, bacon, or fish — all smoked — lift flavors in quiche.

1 9-inch unbaked quiche shell, chilled (p. 56)
5–6 oz. (1½ cups) diced well-flavored ham (avoid water-added plastic ham)
½ lb. (3 cups) white or brown mushrooms, thinly sliced
2 tablespoons butter
⅔ cup quiche onion and garlic (p. 59)
6 oz. (1½ cups) quiche cheese (p. 59)
16 fl. oz. (2 cups) quiche filling (p 58)
finely chopped parsley or dill

1. Melt butter in large frying pan. Quickly sauté mushrooms until cooked through. Season with salt and pepper. Combine mushrooms and diced ham.

2. Follow Quiche Baking Procedure (p. 60)

SPINACH QUICHE

Spinach quiche was our all-season favorite, and frozen spinach eased prep.

1 9-inch unbaked quiche shell, chilled (p. 56)

1 lb. frozen chopped leaf spinach, thawed or fresh spinach,
  blanched

½ teaspoon salt

freshly ground white pepper

freshly grated nutmeg

generous sprinkling of chopped fresh dill (or dry dill weed)

⅔ cup quiche onion and garlic (p. 59)

2 cups quiche filling (p. 58)

6 oz. (1½ cups) quiche cheese (p. 59)

1. Place spinach in a strainer or colander and squeeze out excess water. Season spinach with salt, pepper, nutmeg, and dill. Mix seasoned spinach with onion and garlic.

2. Follow Quiche Baking Procedure (p. 60)

Fresh Tomato Quiche

This one's only for summer.

> 1 9-inch unbaked quiche shell, chilled (p. 56)
> 4–6 fresh ripe tomatoes, 1½ lbs. (locally grown)
> shredded fresh basil or parsley
> ⅔ cup quiche onion and garlic (p. 59)
> 6 oz. (1½ cups) quiche cheese (p. 59)
> 2–2½ cups quiche filling (p. 58)

1. Plunge tomatoes in boiling water for 10 seconds, and slip off skins. Core, halve horizontally, squeeze out seeds. Place halves cut side down, and slice. Toss slices with generous sprinkling of salt and leave 20–30 minutes to release juice. Scoop tomatoes into strainer placed over bowl and shake out juice. Let tomatoes stand in strainer 15 minutes to drain. (Be sure to save drained juice for stocks or soups.) There will be between 1½ and 2 cups of drained tomato slices.

2. See Quiche Baking Procedure (p. 60).

Note: Tomatoes may be combined with diced ham, sautéed mushrooms, or squeezed defrosted cut spinach.

Quiche Notes

LUNCHEON SPECIALS

*E*very hearty luncheon hot dish ran for a full week. We presented a medium-sized serving on a dinner plate alongside a green salad garnished with seasonal fruit. Black bean chili belonged to January; lasagna was on every six–eight weeks; meat or chicken stews also doubled for takeout dinners. These hot luncheon specials attracted a clientele hungry for more than fast-food sandwiches.

Lasagna Bolognese

Over and over I was asked why Mary Jo's lasagna was so "light." The answer lay in the creamy cloud of cheese-laced béchamel on top. For years we rolled homemade pasta for lasagna, but with the arrival of thin no-boil sheets, we took a mini-break.

The Bolognese sauce needs to simmer at least 2 hours and is best prepared a day ahead. I recommend the same cheese mixture used for quiche (a good Swiss mixed with sharp white Cheddar with the addition of grated Parmesan or Romano), because most commercial mozzarella is gummy and tasteless.

Make plenty of lasagna while you are at it. It freezes well, defrosts in a microwave, and a warm square of homemade lasagna nested on a plate of green salad makes a welcome, quick dinner.

To prepare lasagna for 12, you will need 1 9-oz. box no-boil lasagna noodles, 1 recipe Tomato Meat Sauce, 1 recipe Ricotta Filling, 1 recipe Béchamel Sauce, and 6 oz. grated cheese (1½ cups) (Swiss, Cheddar, and Parmesan or Romano).

TOMATO MEAT SAUCE

½ lb. hot Italian sausage

1 lb. lean ground beef

3 tablespoons olive oil

1½ lb. (5-6 cups) onions, peeled and diced

4 oz. (generous ½ cup) carrot, peeled and cut in small dice or grated

4 oz. (¾ cup) celery, cut in small dice

6 cloves garlic, minced

¼–½ teaspoon crushed red pepper

2 teaspoons dry basil (2 tablespoons fresh)

2 teaspoons dry oregano (2 tablespoons fresh)

½ teaspoon dry thyme (1½ teaspoons fresh)

2 bay leaves

4 oz. (½ cup) tomato paste

6 fl. oz. (¾ cup) red wine

2 28-oz. cans peeled whole tomatoes (Italian if possible) or 4 lbs. fresh Italian tomatoes, peeled, seeded, and chopped (save all juice and add)

1 ½–2 teaspoons salt

½ teaspoon sugar

Parmesan cheese rind (optional)

1. Place large stainless steel or non-reactive pot over moderate heat. Crumble in sausage and when it begins to render fat, crumble in beef. Cook both meats through, stirring to prevent caking; scrape into bowl and set aside.

2. Pour olive oil in same pot, add onion, carrot, celery, cover with butter papers, and sweat until limp and translucent, about 15 minutes. Remove paper, stir in minced garlic and crushed dry herbs or chopped fresh herbs.

3. Return meats to pan. Stir in tomato paste; pour in wine and let bubble up. Crush whole tomatoes by hand or in blender and add to meat mixture. Season with salt and sugar, adding cheese rind if available. Bring sauce to simmer and cook slowly at least 2 hours. Add a little water from time to time, if sauce seems too thick. Taste for seasonings; cool and refrigerate until ready to assemble lasagna. Makes 2 generous quarts.

Ricotta Filling

1 lb. whole milk ricotta cheese (15-oz. container is O.K.)
2 eggs
4 oz. (1 cup) grated cheese (Parmesan, Swiss, and white Cheddar mixed)
salt, freshly ground pepper, and nutmeg to taste

Combine above ingredients and taste for seasoning.

Béchamel Sauce

24 fl. oz. (3 cups) whole milk
2 oz. (¼ cup) roux (p. 11)
salt, freshly ground white pepper, nutmeg, and cayenne to taste

1. Heat milk in medium saucepan.

2. Crumble or grate roux into scalding milk. Whisk sauce to light cream as it boils.

3. Remove from heat. Season to taste with salt, white pepper, nutmeg, and cayenne.

White sauce may seem thin; however, it will be just right as it bakes and combines with cheeses.

ASSEMBLY

Choose a deep glass, pottery, or enameled baking dish approximately 10-by-14 inches.

1. Spread 3 cups meat sauce in bottom of dish. Add ½ cup water if sauce seems thick; sauce needs to be thinish, because pasta is dry. Cover sauce with layer of noodles, breaking some into strips to fit pan; do not overlap noodles.

2. Dollop and spread ricotta filling evenly over noodles. Top ricotta with another layer of noodles.

3. Spread another 3 cups meat sauce, thinned with ½ cup water, over noodles. Top with last layer of noodles.

4. Sprinkle over 3 oz. (¾ cup) mixed grated cheese. Pour and spread béchamel sauce over top and sprinkle with last 3 oz. grated cheese.

5. Bake lasagna in a 375°F–400°F oven for 45–50 minutes or until golden and bubbly. Allow to rest at least 15 minutes before serving. Cut into 12 squares.

Note: There should be 2 cups meat sauce remaining. Use this as additional sauce to serve alongside lasagna, or freeze for future pasta saucing.

THE BUILDING

Passersby called Mary Jo's Cuisine a magic cottage. Those who worked there knew it as a funky shop. Its history dated from the nineteen-thirties when it was a creamery. Later, it became an ice-cream factory, then a college snack shop.

At the back end of the building where wide chinks in the cinderblock wall let streams of light into the windowless hull, an antiquated boiler sat on a dirt floor next to ripped bags of hardened concrete. Above creaky wooden steps, an arsenal of electric meters lined the wall flanking the breaker box. The plastic pipe to the floor drain snaked underneath stacks of sofas and mattresses, which the landladies kept in storage for their student apartments. During hot weather the pipes beneath the open cobwebbed rafters dripped with condensation in the dark.

The rear entrance on the north side had once been a garage door for trucks to unload milk cargo, and for years the door's flimsy wooden flap locked with a hasp secured by a long bolt. The day a metal back door with a key was installed, I felt modernized.

A grassy patch surrounded by honeysuckle and hardwood trees lay opposite the driveway to my delivery door. Since drivers often left the door ajar as they dollied in their goods, we were visited each autumn by families of field mice. A cold morning would come when somebody left a bread crust on a counter, and a trail of mouse droppings remained. We'd Clorox the work tops, set traps that evening, and sure enough, I'd find dead mice on the floor the next morning.

From time to time sparrow-sized bats swooped down the range exhaust duct and clung to a dining-room corner or the bottom of a sink to sleep for the day. We learned to scoop them into a cardboard box and plunk them in the woods out back. Our worst trespasser was a squirrel who scrambled through the hood and broke glasses in a manic chase before we finally broom-coaxed it out an open window.

We were fortunate to have a roomy prep area with good natural light. Every day I was grateful for the linoleum-covered wooden floor's gentleness on our legs and feet. Our labyrinthine, low-ceilinged, food-and-wine storage rooms had the crumbly cork walls of deserted coolers. The pasteboard drop-ceiling squares over the hall leading to the freezer often collapsed during heavy rains, and roof water splashed onto trays by the sink. Most of the ceiling tiles were stained and broken — but the health inspector rarely looked up.

I planted an herb garden on the south side that gave us bounteous basil each summer, lush tufts of sorrel in the spring, plus perennial thyme, rosemary, chives, and oregano. Heavy lavender sprays leaned over the front walk, and April daffodils bloomed by the entryway. The north corner harbored a magnificent sixteen-foot apricot tree that I had grown from a Colorado home-place seed.

Our narrow, railcar-shaped dining room presented difficulties when it came to rearranging tables for groups, but we had windows all around. With wall sconces and fairy lights framing the mullioned panes, the room filled with a soft evening glow. After years of wet-mopping the tile dining-room floor, we added a burgundy carpet, which muffled any din and let Mozart's piano sonatas waft through the room.

Ceiling fans whirled throughout summer, and during the evenings we planned menus using minimal heat from the stove. Even so, on warm nights in the crowded room, a guest occasionally blushed with a Zelda Fitzgerald wilt. In winter the floorboard hot water heating wheezed and rattled. Our clunky cash register banged. Yet our glassed refrigerated case displayed an array of fancy cakes and tarts. Wine glasses stood proudly on the doorless shelves of a pierced-tin pie cupboard, and our hand-thrown Irish pottery rose in stacks on Contact paper-lined shelves gleaned from the pizza franchise.

Thousands of nights as I locked the door, I worried about my fridges, freezers, gas pilots, all the wine and food left behind — and always breathed a sigh of thanksgiving when I walked through the shop the next morning.

Basic Tomato Sauce

From the time she was a nursery schooler until she was a vibrant business woman staying at a chic resort in Saint-Tropez, my daughter has always requested noodles and sauce as her meal of choice. This flavorful tomato sauce has been the standard for her freshly cooked pasta, and in the restaurant we kept it on hand for any last-minute vegetarian requests.

The sauce demands little chopping and may also be used for pizza, chicken, and stuffed peppers.

4 tablespoons olive oil
1 lb. (5 cups) onions, peeled and sliced
4 oz. (1 medium) carrot, peeled and thinly sliced
4 oz. (2 small ribs) celery, sliced
4 cloves garlic, sliced
¼ teaspoon crushed red pepper (optional)
2 tablespoons chopped fresh basil (2 teaspoons dry)
2 tablespoons chopped fresh oregano (2 teaspoons dry)
1½ teaspoons chopped fresh thyme (½ teaspoon dry)
2 bay leaves
1 oz. (2 tablespoons) tomato paste
4 fl. oz. (½ cup) red or white wine
2 28-oz. cans peeled whole or diced tomatoes (Italian if possible) or in season
   4–5 lbs. ripe tomatoes (see Note)
1½ teaspoons salt
½ teaspoon sugar
Parmesan cheese rind if available

1. Warm olive oil in large stainless or enameled pot and gently sweat onions, carrot, and celery. This will take at least 30 minutes; vegetables must become limp, translucent, and reduced.

2. Add garlic, red pepper, and fresh or crushed dry herbs. Sauté until fragrant. Stir in tomato paste and sauté a few minutes. Add wine; let bubble up and add crushed tomatoes, salt, sugar, and cheese rind. Add 24 fl. oz. (3 cups) water, bring to a simmer and cook 2–3 hours. Make sure carrots are soft. Check seasonings, adding more salt or sugar if needed.

3. While still warm, pass sauce through food mill to break up vegetables and remove tomato seeds, or purée in food processor and rub through coarse sieve. Makes 2 quarts.

This sauce may be refrigerated for a week, or frozen in pint cartons.

Note: In high summer when the herb garden is lush and baskets of ripened tomatoes wait in farmers' markets, make up pots of this sauce to freeze for winter. To use garden-ripe tomatoes; wash, core, and cut tomatoes in half around the equator. No need to peel. Squeeze halves to release seeds. Pass seedy pulp through a strainer. Reserve juice and discard seeds. Add halved tomatoes and juice to sautéed aromatic vegetables. Do not add extra water.

Gather a bouquet of garden herbs: 1 sprig rosemary, 4 sprigs thyme, 4 sprigs oregano, and 3 leafy stems basil. Omit dry herbs. Tie herb bouquet with kitchen string and immerse in simmering sauce. After sauce has reduced and thickened, cool slightly, squeeze out herb bouquet, and discard. Pass sauce through a food mill to remove tomato skins, or purée in processor and pass through a coarse sieve. This sauce is so good you may want to eat it with a spoon for dessert.

Vegetarian Lasagna

This lasagna always pleased vegetarian diners. Vegetable lasagna can be made with broccoli, mushrooms, zucchini, onions, and peppers, as well as spinach.

1 quart (4 cups) Basic Tomato Sauce (p. 78)
1 9-oz. package no-boil lasagna noodles
1 recipe Ricotta Filling (p. 74)
1 16-oz. package frozen, chopped leaf spinach, defrosted
6 oz. chopped onion (I medium, about 1½ cups)
1 tablespoon olive oil
2 cloves garlic, finely chopped
1 tablespoon chopped fresh dill (optional)
salt, freshly ground white pepper, freshly grated nutmeg, and cayenne
6 oz. (1½ cups) grated mixed cheese (Swiss, white Cheddar, Parmesan)
4 cups béchamel sauce (p. 74) using 4 cups milk and
   2½ oz. (5 tablespoons) roux

1. Gently sweat chopped onion in olive oil until transparent and soft; add garlic and cook a few more minutes. Place spinach in large strainer and, using your hand, squeeze excess water from spinach. In medium bowl, mix spinach with softened onion, garlic, dill, one cup of prepared béchamel sauce, salt, pepper, nutmeg to taste.

2. Build lasagna in a 10-by-14-inch rectangular baking dish. Spread 3 cups tomato sauce in bottom of pan. Make sure tomato sauce is not too thick, adding a little water if necessary. Arrange noodles over tomato sauce, breaking them when necessary to fill in spaces. Do not overlap noodles.

3. Dollop ricotta filling over noodles by spoonfuls and spread to an even layer. Arrange another layer of noodles over ricotta.

4. Spoon and spread spinach mixture evenly over noodles. Top with final layer of noodles.

5. Sprinkle 3 oz. (¾ cup) grated cheese over noodles. Pour and spread remaining 3 cups béchamel sauce over cheese and sprinkle 3 oz. cheese evenly over top. Preheat oven to 375°F.

6. Bake lasagna 45–55 minutes or until top is lightly browned and lasagna is slightly puffed. Cool 15 minutes and cut into 12 squares. Serve with extra tomato sauce if desired.

Carbonnades Flamandes

Pascale came from Belgium and enjoyed serving her country's national dish. Prepared ahead, the stew has even more flavor when reheated the next day. Substitute Irish stout for beer and you have a feast for St. Paddy's.

2 lbs. trimmed boneless beef chuck
1 oz. (2 tablespoons) butter
2 tablespoons olive oil
1½ lbs. onions, peeled and sliced (3 medium large onions)
2 cloves garlic, finely chopped
1 bay leaf
large sprig fresh thyme (½ teaspoon dry)
a little grated nutmeg
⅛ teaspoon crushed red pepper (optional)
12 fl. oz. (1½ cups) bottle dark beer or ale
2 fl. oz. (¼ cup) dry red wine (optional)
1 tablespoon wine vinegar
salt and pepper
1 generous teaspoon Dijon mustard (optional)

1. Trim beef, cut into 2-inch chunks, season with salt, pepper and allow to rest overnight in refrigerator or at least ½ hour at room temperature.

2. Heat ½ butter and oil in heavy frying pan. Brown beef carefully. Remove browned meat to heavy braising pan, enameled cast iron suggested.

3. Add remaining butter and oil to frying pan. Sweat sliced onions covered with butter papers until reduced. Raise heat, uncover, and continue to sauté onions until golden brown. This will take 20–30 minutes and will add rich character to sauce. Add garlic and cook until fragrant. Add beer, red wine, and bring to simmer. Pour beer and onion mixture over beef. Add herbs, nutmeg, salt, and pepper.

4. Cover and simmer on stovetop or braise slowly in 325°F oven for 2 hours or until meat is very tender. Near end of cooking, add vinegar and allow to simmer 15 minutes. Mix mustard into 2 tablespoons cooking juices, and pour over casserole just before serving. When finished there will be 1½ pounds of lean, cooked meat and 2 cups of richly flavored onion sauce. There is no need to thicken gravy when serving with boiled potatoes, egg noodles, or crusty bread. Present with braised carrots and buttered cabbage. Serves 4–6.

Note: If you prefer a thickened sauce, remove chunks of meat and grate nut-sized lump of cold roux over simmering sauce and whisk to blend. Or, else dissolve 2 teaspoons cornstarch in 2 tablespoons cold water and whisk starch solution into bubbling sauce.

CHICKEN PAPRIKASH

A popular cook-ahead braised chicken from eastern Europe—good with noodles or boiled potatoes.

1 3½–4-lb. chicken cut up
2 tablespoons olive oil or rendered duck fat
1 large onion (10 oz.) (2 cups), peeled and chopped
1 large sweet red, yellow, or green pepper, diced (about 2 cups)
3 cloves garlic, finely chopped
½–1 teaspoon finely chopped red or green chili (optional)
1 tablespoon chopped fresh marjoram or oregano (1 teaspoon dry)
2 teaspoons chopped fresh thyme leaves (½ teaspoon dry)
2 tablespoons Hungarian paprika
8 fl. oz. (1 cup) chicken stock (plus more for sauce)
6 oz. (⅔ cup) sour cream
8 oz. (3 cups) mushrooms, sliced and sautéed in 1 tablespoon butter or oil
lemon juice to taste, flour or corn starch (optional)

1. Trim chicken of excess fat, skin, and non-meaty bones; season with salt and refrigerate overnight or allow to stand at room temperature ½ hour. Prepare all vegetables and herbs.

2. Heat 1 tablespoon oil or duck fat in large iron skillet, and brown chicken pieces over high heat. Remove chicken pieces to heavy braising pan such as an enameled cast-iron casserole. Make sure legs, thighs, and wings are on bottom of braising pan and breast portions on top. Pour all browning fat from skillet, reduce heat, add 1 tablespoon fresh fat or oil, and gently sauté chopped onion and pepper until limp and tender. Add garlic, chili, herbs; sauté a few minutes. Add paprika, stirring constantly, and sauté until paprika smells fragrant. Add chicken stock, and pour paprika mixture over chicken in casserole.

3. Preheat oven to 325°F (alternatively the casserole may be simmered on stovetop). Bake or simmer casserole 20 minutes. Remove breasts and test for doneness. Breast meat cooks faster and should register 140°F on an instant-read thermometer. Continue cooking dark meat and wings another 20 minutes.

4. When chicken is tender, remove from braising casserole. Skim as much fat from surface as possible. (Notice that this fat is brilliant red and tastes delicious; it contains most of the paprika.) If you are comfortable using this paprika fat, place 2 tablespoons in small skillet and cook with 2 tablespoons of flour to form roux. (If you do not want to use paprika fat, you may substitute butter or olive oil. Sauce may also be thickened with a tablespoon of cornstarch dissolved in a spoonful of water.)

5. Bring sauce to simmer; crumble in roux, whisk, and cook to smooth gravy. Add more stock if needed. Allow to simmer a few minutes before adding prepared mushrooms and stir in sour cream. Taste for seasoning, adding a few drops of lemon juice to lift flavor. Return chicken to sauce. Serves 4–6.

THE GOOD TABLE

Patrons entering a restaurant almost always move in the same direction.

We noticed our customers moved away from the kitchen toward a window. We had a table in such a spot near the back of the dining room. We soon called it "The Good Table," though it was really no better than any other. The disgruntled server had to walk farther, especially when guests asked for extras one at a time.

My staff all knew that the best spot was the four-top up front. There, our faithful regulars, a savvy European couple, often sat. As Lisa confided, "I choose to sit near the seat of power," in sight of the cooking and the chef's eye! La Bonne Place!

CHICKEN MASALA

This is the curry method I learned in the kitchens of several quiet Indian women who worked through the morning each day to prepare an extensive meal. Even now when I sit on a small stool, the grinding stone between my feet, I pound ginger and chilis to a paste, recalling Heradia's dusty shop, the jangle of Pardahn's household, and the patient sweetness of Shagufta Singh.

3 ½ lbs. whole chicken, cut-up, or 2½ lbs. chicken legs and thighs

4–5 tablespoons vegetable oil (or 2 tablespoons butter plus oil)

1 3-inch coiled stick Ceylon cinnamon or 1 regular cinnamon stick

5 whole cloves

3 whole green cardamoms

2 large onions (1¼ lbs.), thinly sliced (4–5 cups)

2 oz. (½ cup) fresh ginger, peeled and sliced

1 oz. (6–8 cloves, ¼ cup) garlic, peeled and sliced

2 or 3 green chilis (cayenne or serrano), seeds intact, 1 sliced, 2 whole
    generous teaspoon salt

1 tablespoon ground coriander

2 teaspoons ground cumin

2 teaspoons ground turmeric

1½ teaspoon garam masala (p. 13)

¼ teaspoon cayenne pepper

1 tablespoon curry powder (optional)

1 14½ oz. can good quality canned tomatoes or 1 lb. fresh tomatoes in season,
    peeled, seeded, and chopped

1 tablespoon tomato paste (optional)

1 cup water

fresh lime juice and cilantro

1. Pull off as much skin as possible from chicken, trim excess fat, pat dry with paper towels, and season with salt. Cover and refrigerate overnight or leave ½ hour at room temperature.

2. Heat 4 tablespoons oil (or 2 tablespoons each butter and oil) in enameled casserole or heavy stewing pot; add whole spices and sliced onion. Sauté

gently for 30–40 minutes or until onions have reduced to deep golden brown. Meanwhile, prepare crushed "green spices" and measure all dry spices into a small cup.

3. Grind sliced chili with ginger and garlic. To grind these green spices in a mortar, begin with sliced chili and pinch of salt. When chili is mashed to paste, add ½ ginger and another pinch salt. Continue with remaining ginger, and finally add garlic. Crush thoroughly, pounding and grinding against the stone to produce ½ cup ginger mash.

To grind green spices in a blender, place chopped ginger, garlic, and chili in blender jar. Add ¼-cup water and pulse to smooth purée.

4. When onions have reduced and browned, add ginger mash and continue to sauté, stirring constantly until seasonings smell cooked and any water has evaporated. Sprinkle in mixed dry spices and continue stirring until mixture is delightfully fragrant. At this point seasoning base will have reduced to a dark lump smaller than a baseball. Gradually blend in chopped tomatoes, tomato paste, and water. Add 1 or 2 whole chilis if desired. Simmer sauce, covered, 30 minutes. Remove whole chilis when sauce seems spicy enough.

5. Meanwhile, lightly brown chicken pieces in 1 tablespoon oil and add to sauce in casserole. (Discard fat in frying pan, deglaze pan with water, and add deglazing liquid to curry.) Take care to place dark meat on bottom and breast pieces on top, because white meat will cook faster and will need to be removed before dark meat is ready. (This step is optional. Many cooks add raw chicken to the prepared curry sauce for cooking; however, the effort of browning will add depth of flavor to the finished dish.) Cover and bake in moderate oven or simmer on stovetop. Breast meat will be ready in 20–30 minutes; dark meat will take 45–50 minutes.

6. When chicken is tender, skim excess fat if necessary and taste sauce for seasoning, adding fresh lemon or lime juice and generous amount of chopped cilantro. Serve with Lentil Rice (p. 90) or steamed rice and Cucumber Raita (p. 48).

Note: For a typical variation, simmer 1 large peeled, diced potato along with chicken, and just before serving, sprinkle in 1 cup frozen peas.

Black Bean Chili

When winter's chill blasted our windowpanes, nothing warmed bodies and souls like this fragrant Black Bean Chili. We served it thick like a stew with a scoop of brown rice, a dollop of sour cream, and salsa of chopped serrano, cilantro, red onion with lime juice.

1 lb. black beans
2 oz. chunk fatty bacon (optional)
3 oz. mixed dried Mexican chilis (4 anchos and 4 pasillas recommended)
2 lbs. mixed lean beef and pork
5 tablespoons oil, pork dripping, or duck fat
1 lb. onions, chopped or diced (3 cups)
6–8 cloves garlic, minced
1 small lemon sliced, seeded, and cut into small dice (½ cup)
¼ teaspoon cayenne
2 teaspoons paprika
1 tablespoon ground cumin
1 tablespoon ground coriander
1 teaspoon crushed dry red chili
1 oz. (2 tablespoons) tomato paste
1 14½ oz. can tomatoes, chopped (or 1 lb. summer tomatoes)
1 fl. oz. (2 tablespoons) cider vinegar
12 fl. oz. (1½ cups, 1 can or bottle) beer
2 bay leaves
1 teaspoon oregano
2 dried chipotle chilis (optional)
salt

1. Check black beans for stones; rinse, cover with water, and soak overnight. Drain, cover with fresh water, and simmer beans with bacon until very tender.

2. Wipe any dust off chilis with dry cloth. Warm and soften whole chilis by turning them from side to side on hot frying pan until soft and fragrant; do not burn. Break off stems, split open sides, shake out seeds, and pull away membranes. Tear chilis into quarter-sized (25¢) pieces (there will be 2 loose cups).

Cover chilis with 2 cups boiling water. Weight chilis with saucer topped with glass of water. Soak chilis 20 minutes. Purée chilis and soaking water in blender. Press chili pulp through strainer to remove skins. You should have 1¾ cups of thick dark red chili purée. This purée gives the chili real character.

3. Cut beef and pork into ½-inch cubes—or use coarsely ground meats. If you buy regular ground meat, choose lean beef and Italian sausage meat. Season meat generously with salt. Brown meats in hot, heavy frying pan filmed with pork or duck fat or oil. Set aside.

4. Heat 4 tablespoons fat or oil in heavy frying pan. Add onions and cook gently until tender and golden. Add chopped garlic and sauté until fragrant. Measure cayenne, paprika, cumin, coriander, and crushed red pepper into small cup. Add dry spices all at once and stir constantly to sauté slightly. Add tomato paste and continue to sauté. Add red chili purée and stir constantly while chili purée sputters and bubbles. Scrape chili mixture into stainless steel or enameled iron braising pan; deglaze frying pan with ½ beer. Mix in cooked meats.

5. Add lemon, tomatoes, remaining beer, vinegar, bay leaves, oregano, and salt. If you desire a spicier chili, tuck in two dry chipotle chilis, or add more crushed red pepper. After mixture comes to simmer, cover and cook slowly in moderate oven or continue cooking on stovetop. Simmer chili at least 2 hours or until meats are tender and sauce is deeply flavored. Add drained cooked beans (save bean water in case chili gets too thick and needs extra liquid), and continue simmering another ½ hour. Remove chipotles before serving. There should be 3 quarts of thick chili. Serves 6–8.

LENTIL RICE

1½ cup basmati rice
½ cup small pink lentils (masoor dal)
½ teaspoon salt
3 cups soaking water

Combine rice and lentils in large bowl. Cover with cold water; swirl gently with fingertips until water becomes cloudy. Drain water and repeat. Cover with fresh water and allow to soak 20 minutes. Drain water, retaining 3 cups soaking water. Combine lentils, rice, salt, and retained water in heavy pan with tight-fitting lid; stir to dissolve salt. Bring to boil and simmer 10 minutes or until water is absorbed. Place cloth napkin or tea towel underneath pot lid to absorb moisture and allow to rest 10 minutes before serving. This same method may also be used with brown rice and urhad dal (hulled black gram), using more cooking water and longer cooking time.

Note: For plain steamed basmati rice, omit lentils, reduce retained soaking water to 2 cups. Follow procedure for lentil rice.

Luncheon Notes

BREADS

Homemade bread was a priority in the restaurant. Our gas-fired Blodgett oven allowed us to bake directly on the hearth floor. Gentle heat coming from the bottom of the gas oven is the best for light, crisp breads, but any conventional oven will produce genuine loaves and rolls. Yeast baking has been my lifelong commitment.

BALLYMALOE BROWN YEAST BREAD

This is an American adaptation of the famous Brown Yeast Bread prepared at the Ballymaloe House in Shanagarry, County Cork, Ireland. I delighted in this bread from the first bite in 1983 and made it daily for Mary Jo's Cuisine. I hope never to live without it.

Anyone can make this bread. It is not kneaded; it is quick and practically foolproof. Remember that yeast is a living organism and to stay active it must not get too hot or too cold. Choose whole-wheat flour that is stone ground from hard wheat. Supermarket whole-wheat flour is usually finely ground and can be given more texture with the addition of bran, wheat germ, ground flax, oatmeal, or cracked wheat. If you add any of these ingredients, be sure to remove an equal amount of flour from the basic measure. A scale is helpful.

16 fl. oz. (2 cups) lukewarm water
1 tablespoon dark molasses
1 packet active dry yeast (2¼ teaspoons)
1 lb. (3¼ cups) whole wheat flour
1 teaspoon salt
tiny pinch ground ginger (optional)
lightly toasted brown sesame seeds (optional)

1. Dissolve molasses in warm water and sprinkle yeast over top. Set aside and allow yeast to "sponge" into thick foam on top of water. Meanwhile, combine flour, salt, and ginger in medium bowl; make a well in center. When yeast has dissolved and foamed, mix it into water and pour liquid into flour. Mix with your clean hand until all flour has moistened into damp dough. It should be the consistency of a thick muffin mixture.

2. Scrape your hand clean. Cover bowl loosely with tea towel; set it in a warm place and allow to rise for 20–30 minutes or until dough is light. (If time does not permit this first rising, go straight to step 3. In Ireland this first rising is omitted; however, I have found it helpful with our flour.)

3. Butter or grease 1 large loaf pan or two 3½-by-7½ inch loaf pans. After dough has risen, stir it down with your hand and scoop dough into pans. Smooth top with damp fingers; sprinkle with sesame seeds; cover with tea towel and set aside to rise. Preheat oven to 450°F. If dough half fills pan, it should rise until it comes to top edge. This second rising takes 20–30 minutes, depending on warmth of room.

4. Bake loaves for 25–40 minutes, depending on their size or until nicely browned. Remove loaves from pans at once (the loaf should sound hollow when knocked with a fist). Return loaves to oven without pans for further crisping if desired. Allow bread to cool on wire racks before slicing. This bread slices with ease when fully cool, but it will be sticky inside if sliced while warm.

Brown bread makes the best breakfast toast and is excellent as a canapé base.

FRENCH BREAD

A tried and true crusty bread that can easily be made at home without any special baking equipment. Use baguette form pans if you have them or make free-form baguettes, balls, or smaller rolls. You must have bread flour for this dough. A straightedged razor blade and a plastic spray bottle are two useful pieces of equipment. This is the bread no Frenchman can live without, a sharp contrast to American gummy white bread.

16 fl. oz. (2 cups) lukewarm water
¼ teaspoon sugar
pinch ground ginger (optional)
1 packet active dry yeast (2¼ teaspoons)
1½ lbs. (5 cups) bread flour
2½ teaspoons salt

1. Place water, sugar, and ginger in deep warm mixing bowl. Sprinkle yeast over top and allow to dissolve and "sponge." Measure bread flour and set aside 4 oz. (scant cup) to add while kneading. When yeast has dissolved, stir in 1¼ lbs. flour to moisten. Clean off spoon, sprinkle salt over top of dough (do not mix in salt until kneading because salt slows yeast action), cover with tea towel, and allow to rest 15 minutes. This resting time lets flour absorb moisture, making kneading time more efficient.

2. a) If you plan to knead using a dough hook in an electric mixer, combine dough in mixing bowl and stir in all the flour at the beginning; sprinkle salt over top. After dough has rested, use hook to knead for 10 minutes (knead dough in 2 batches if mixer is strained). Clean insides of bowl well with stiff plastic scraper working all bits into dough. Cover top of bowl with plastic wrap.

b) To knead by hand, dust some reserved flour onto clean, smooth surface, and scrape dough out onto floured kneading place. Knead steadily for 10 minutes. Incorporate last 4 oz. of flour into dough as you knead. The well-kneaded dough should feel satiny and springy when patted, "like a baby's bottom." Return dough to scraped-clean mixing bowl; cover tightly with plastic wrap or large plastic bag, and set aside in warm place to rise until doubled in size. If time permits, punch dough down and allow to rise 30 minutes or until almost doubled again.

3. Punch down risen dough and scrape it out onto flour-dusted, clean, flat surface. Using knife or dough scraper, cut dough in half for large free-form loaves, in thirds for baguettes, or into 12 lumps for hard rolls. Turn cut sides of lumps in to retain satiny surface tension on outer layer of loaves. Form round even balls with pinched-together edges underneath, or roll into long sausage shapes for baguettes. Place shaped dough on flat baking sheet lightly dusted with flour or lined with parchment baking paper. Cover loaves or rolls with tea towel and set aside in warm place to rise. When loaves have almost doubled in size, preheat oven to 450°F.

4. When rolls have doubled in volume and oven is ready, slash top of each roll or make diagonal slashes on large loaves with razor blade or small sharp knife. Mist slashed loaves with water and place in hot oven. Bake rolls 15–20 minutes, larger loaves 25–30 minutes or until deeply golden brown and until they sound hollow when knocked with a fist. Remove to cooling rack.

Note: If French bread is not to be used the same day it is baked, seal in plastic bags and freeze as soon as thoroughly cool. To recrisp and warm, take bread directly from freezer to a low oven or allow to defrost at room temperature and recrisp in a moderate oven. Do not wrap bread when reheating; simply place baked loaf on oven rack.

A baker's trick for deepening flavor: Remove a 2 oz. lump of dough before shaping loaves. Place dough lump in small plastic container and pop it in freezer. Next time you bake bread, defrost the dough ball an hour before mixing fresh dough. Add the room-temperature lump of dough to water and softening yeast for the new batch. Continue bread-making process.

Scones

These are soft, floury—real Irish or English—scones. Try this small recipe to learn the technique, then double the amounts for a larger batch and store some in the freezer.

8 oz. (1¾ cups) all-purpose flour
1 tablespoon sugar
scant ½ teaspoon salt
2 teaspoons baking powder
1½ oz. (3 tablespoons) unsalted butter
1 egg
3½ oz. (½ cup minus 1 tablespoon) milk
1 oz. (¼ cup) currants or raisins (optional)
1 tablespoon sugar for sprinkling

1. Preheat oven to 450°F. Have ready a baking sheet lightly sprinkled with flour or lined with parchment.

2. Beat egg; remove 1 tablespoon and save in small cup for egg wash. Combine remaining egg with milk, whisking together.

3. Sift together flour, 1 tablespoon sugar, salt, and baking powder. Cut butter into slices and rub into flour with your fingertips.

4. Make a well in center of dry ingredients. Add milk mixture and begin to mix with your hand, sprinkling in raisins or currants. Once dry mixture is thoroughly moistened, scrape scone dough out onto lightly floured surface. Knead lightly, only 3 or 4 turns to bring the dough together. Scrape dough from your hands and pat or roll to circle ¾ inch thick. Cut into 7 2½-inch scones, re-rolling scraps. Place scones on baking sheet, brush tops with reserved egg wash, and sprinkle with sugar.

5. Bake in preheated oven 15 minutes or until lightly brown. Serve warm with butter and jam or whipped cream and jam. Scones may be frozen and reheated.

Note: If your baking powder is not fresh, make your own by combining baking soda and cream of tartar. Mix ½ teaspoon cream of tartar with ¼ teaspoon baking soda to equal leavening of 1 teaspoon baking powder.

For this recipe use 1 teaspoon cream of tartar + ½ teaspoon soda.

THE CRATE

I can't remember when I started carrying the crate. It must have come into my possession, borrowed from the Trauth Dairy, as I picked up four or six quarts of their heavy fresh cream each week. Printed on its green side were the words, "WARNING. Use by other than reg. owner prohibited by law, $500 fine max." The crate carried my checkbook, cash box, handbag, spiral notebook with work orders, bits of food to take home, dishes to return, and milk or eggs that I might have collected along the way. Balanced on my left hip like a toddler, the crate came out of the house with me in the morning and out of the shop at night.

Restaurant-quality Trauth cream was richer, fresher, and not the usual "long life" cream, which is the only kind available in most supermarkets nowadays. I bought the cream from local mini-marts willing to add it onto their orders. The last few years included a Friday morning pickup at a nearby florist where the cream waited in the flower cooler. Phyllis brought it in from her husband's corner grocery, and I collected the cream, left a check, and bartered cake for posies to arrange in the small vases that adorned my tables.

Cinnamon Rolls

We baked these soft cinnamon rolls before lunch, and our patrons bought them to take home. This basic sweet dough is easy to manage, especially if you have a stand mixer with a dough hook.

1 package (2¼ teaspoons) active dry yeast

8 fl. oz. (1 cup) lukewarm milk

1½ oz. (3 tablespoons) sugar

pinch powdered ginger (optional)

1 teaspoon salt

2 eggs at room temperature

1 lb. (3½ cups) bread flour

2 oz. (½ stick) soft butter

1 oz. (2 tablespoons) very soft butter

3 oz. (scant packed ½ cup) brown sugar

1 teaspoon cinnamon

3 oz. (⅔ cup) raisins

3 oz. (generous ¾ cup) powdered sugar

1½ tablespoons milk

1. In mixing bowl dissolve yeast in warm milk. Beat eggs in small bowl; remove 2 tablespoons and set aside in small cup for egg wash. When yeast foams, add sugar, salt, ginger, eggs, and flour; stir to combine and moisten flour. Cover bowl with towel and allow flour to thoroughly absorb liquid for 10–15 minutes.

2. Place dough on hook and begin to knead. When dough becomes neat ball, add 2 oz. soft butter in several pinches. Continue to knead at least 10 minutes or until dough is smooth and satiny. Resist adding any more flour than absolutely necessary. Dough must be soft for light rolls.

3. Remove dough from hook. Cover bowl with plastic wrap and allow dough to rise until double in volume, 1–2 hours depending on temperature. Uncover, punch down, cover again, and allow to rise for another 30 minutes.

4. Have ready 2 buttered 8- or 9-inch round cake pans or 1 large rectangular baking pan. Thoroughly combine brown sugar and cinnamon.

5. Roll dough on lightly floured clean, flat surface to 18-by-9-inch rectangle. Spread with soft butter, dust evenly with cinnamon and brown sugar, and sprinkle raisins over sugar. Roll up from long side of rectangle. Pinch edges of roll, and rock back and forth gently to even out. Use 10-inch section of heavy cotton string to "tie-cut" the log into 12 1½-inch cinnamon "snails." Place rolls in prepared pans, cover with a tea towel, and allow to rise in warm place for 30–40 minutes or until doubled and light. Meanwhile, preheat oven to 350°F. Before baking, brush tops of rolls lightly with reserved egg wash. Bake 25 minutes or until golden brown.

6. While rolls are baking, mix 3 oz. (generous ¾ cup) powdered sugar with 1½ tablespoons milk to make glaze. Use pastry brush to ice and glaze warm rolls as soon as they come out of oven. Makes 12 large cinnamon rolls.

HOT CROSS BUNS

1 packet (2¼ teaspoons) active dry yeast
pinch ground ginger (optional)
8 fl. oz. (1 cup) lukewarm whole milk
2½ oz. (⅓ cup) sugar
2 eggs at room temperature
1 teaspoon salt
½ teaspoon ground cinnamon
½ teaspoon grated nutmeg
¼ teaspoon ground allspice
1 lb. (3½ cups) bread flour
3 oz. (6 tablespoons) unsalted butter, softened
4–5 oz. (1 cup) mixed raisins and currants
2 tablespoons diced homemade candied orange or lemon peel (optional)
egg wash* and powdered sugar glaze (p. 101)

1. Sprinkle yeast and ginger over warm milk in mixing bowl. Give yeast a few minutes to dissolve. Add sugar, eggs, salt, spices, and whisk together. Add bread flour; stir to combine and allow to rest 10–15 minutes for flour to absorb moisture.

2. Knead dough using dough hook on standing electric mixer, or scrape dough onto lightly floured flat surface and knead by hand. Resist temptation to add any more than very little additional flour. Knead for 3–4 minutes; then knead in soft butter 2 tablespoons at a time. Continue kneading for total of 10 minutes. Dough now should be soft and silky. Cover and allow dough to rest 10–20 minutes. Work in fruits until evenly distributed through dough. Place dough in mixing bowl, cover, and allow to rise in warm place until double in volume.

3. Punch down dough and scrape out onto lightly floured flat surface. Using dough cutter or long knife, cut patted-out dough into 15–16 even lumps. Each piece will weigh about 2½ oz. Shape each lump into a nice round bun and place on lightly greased or parchment-lined baking sheet. Cover with tea towel and allow buns to rise until double in size.

4. Preheat oven to 350°F. Brush buns with egg wash and bake for 20 minutes or until golden brown.

5. For glazed buns brush lightly with powdered sugar icing (p. 101) while still hot. To make crosses let buns cool, then pipe or drip an icing cross over each bun. Makes 16. Hot Cross Buns disappear fast but also freeze well.

* To make egg wash, beat a whole egg (save what's left in the freezer for later baking).

IF YE HAVE NO DAUGHTERS, GIVE THEM TO YOUR SONS.
ONE A PENNY, TWO A PENNY, HOT CROSS BUNS.

Alive in Mother Goose, Hot Cross Buns are now nearly extinct in popular culture. Traditionally they were made on Good Friday as a pre-Easter treat. These lightly sweetened spiced buns studded with raisins and currants are welcome in spring.

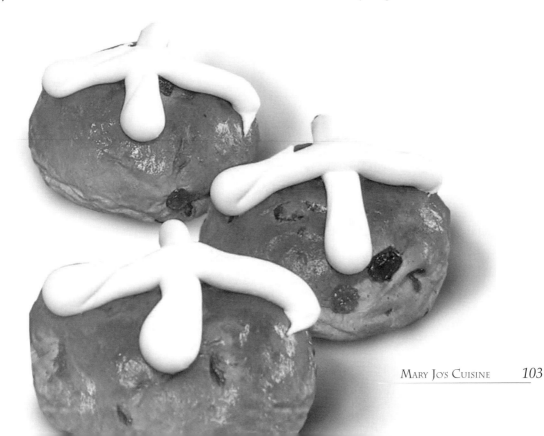

STOLLEN

Stollen is the hallmark of European holiday baking. More of a cake than a bread, it combines a light buttery brioche with fruit and marzipan. I baked 30–50 stollen each Christmas Eve at Mary Jo's Cuisine. You can prepare the fruit one day, the marzipan filling another day, make the dough one day, and bake the stollen the next day. This scaled-down recipe works perfectly in a home stand mixer with a dough hook and will make 1 very large stollen or 2 medium-sized cakes.

8 oz. (1⅓ cups) mixed dried and candied fruit (golden raisins, currants, dried apricots, dried pineapple, homemade candied orange peel, candied cherries)
2 tablespoons brandy

4 oz. (½ cup) almond paste
1 tablespoon sugar (omit if using crumbs)
1 tablespoon egg white
1½ oz. ground almonds <u>or</u> fine, dry, plain cake or cookie crumbs, scant ½ cup (use shortbread, butter cookies, or pound cake)
⅛ teaspoon almond extract (optional)

1 packet (2¼ teaspoons) active dry yeast
4 fl. oz. (½ cup) whole milk
pinch ground ginger (optional)
4 oz. (1 spooned-in cup minus 1 tablespoon) bread flour

grated rind ½ lemon
2 oz. (5 tablespoons) sugar
4 oz. (1 stick) softened unsalted butter
2 eggs at room temperature
¾ teaspoon salt
9 oz. (2 spooned-in cups) bread flour
melted unsalted butter and powdered sugar

1. Two days before baking, gather dried and candied fruit. Cut all larger fruit to size of raisins. Place cut mixed fruit in bowl; sprinkle over brandy. Cover with plastic wrap and set aside at room temperature to macerate.

2. Prepare marzipan filling. Crumble almond paste in bowl. Add sugar and work with your fingertips until almond paste is sandy. Add crumbs or ground almonds and continue to combine until mixture looks like cornmeal. Add egg white and mix to soft clay. Taste; add almond extract if desired. Knead and shape into log. It should weigh 6 oz. Wrap and set aside.

3. Prepare dough. Heat milk to lukewarm; pour into medium bowl; sprinkle yeast over milk, adding pinch of ground ginger. Cover with tea towel and allow yeast to soften in milk (3–5 minutes). Add 4 oz. flour and mix to soft dough. Cover again and allow this thick batter to rise 40–50 minutes or until light and bubbly. This mixture is called a sponge.

4. While sponge is developing, grate lemon into mixing bowl. Add 2 oz. sugar and work lemon rind into sugar with your fingertips. Add softened butter to bowl; beat with paddle until butter is creamed. Beat in eggs one at a time. Mixture will look curdled. Mix in salt. Remove paddle and change to dough hook, or prepare to knead by hand.

5. When sponge has risen, scrape it into egg and butter mixture. Add 9 oz. bread flour. Knead by machine or work on flat surface until dough is soft and satiny (10 minutes). Place dough in mixing bowl; cover and allow to rise at room temperature until doubled and light.

6. Punch down dough and scrape it onto clean flat surface. Pat dough into large rectangle. Strew macerated fruit evenly over surface. Roll dough up like a jellyroll and continue to knead until fruit seems distributed throughout. The paste will seem ropy and sticky at times, but try to avoid adding extra flour; simply rub dough off your hands onto the lump. Cover dough with tea towel, allow to rest a few minutes, and then knead again. When fruit is evenly mixed into dough, scrape mass back into clean bowl, and cover tightly with plastic wrap, or place dough in large plastic container with tight-fitting lid.

7. Place fruited dough in fridge and allow it to rise overnight. Dough will expand a bit and then will become solid due to butter hardening.

8. The next morning pat cold dough into large oval on lightly floured surface, or divide dough in half, shaping into 2 smaller ovals. With rolling pin, flatten oval to ½-inch thickness, and crease at center lengthwise. Elongate marzipan log and place it along crease. Do not let marzipan extend to edge of dough. Fold one long side of oval over the other to form large Parker House roll shape.

9. Place shaped stollen on parchment-lined baking sheet. Cover with tea towel and allow to rise until double in size (1½–2 hours). It doesn't matter how long it takes; check stollen every quarter hour to note progress. Take care not to let surface dry; it may be necessary to cover rising stollen with large plastic bag to keep in moisture.

10. When dough is almost ready, preheat oven to 350°F. Before placing in oven, mist surface with water from household spray bottle. Bake stollen 30–40 minutes or until golden brown. As soon as stollen is taken from oven, brush top liberally with melted butter, and as butter is absorbed into crust, generously sift powdered sugar over top. Allow stollen to cool on wire rack.

11. When stollen is cool, wrap in plastic film or seal in plastic bag. Makes one large cake, 18-by-9 inches, or two 12-by-5-inch cakes. Stollen may be used straightaway, or it may be held for a few days before slicing, or it may be frozen. Stollen is best with morning coffee, afternoon tea, or late evening port.

Note: If you prefer to omit the marzipan filling, proceed with the recipe, shaping the dough as directed or use medium buttered loaf pans or brioche molds. The candied fruit may be omitted and the raisins/currants increased.

BREAD NOTES

DINNER MAINS

Our weekend dinners were European in style. We used the French prix fixe menu model (the price for dinner included all four courses). The main choices each evening comprised one meat, one fish, one chicken, and a vegetarian entrée on request. Each main course plate included a complementary sauce, starch, and an assortment of vegetables. The dinner mains changed every three weeks.

A key to the success of the fixed menu was keeping servings moderate, so guests felt comfortable throughout the meal. We gave our diners time. We opposed the policy of hurrying people out to fill the tables again. Our mission was to let people dine well in a peaceful place. We always hoped dinner at Mary Jo's lifted spirits and sent folks out into the world with good will.

BEEF BOURGUIGNON

Mary Jo's Cuisine popularized Old World braises. These classics may be prepared ahead and always taste better the next day. They use inexpensive cuts of meat, but demand skill and time. A great stew is often more of a treat than a steak because few people cook this way anymore.

We always served Beef Bourguignon for big celebration weekends. Even during the years when the public ate less red meat, this dish remained a sell-out. Old-fashioned, often called a French pot roast, it is never out of style.

A few guidelines for braising: 1. Allow three days to manage the dish with ease. 2. Trim, cut, and season meat the night before. 3. Use less rather than more liquid in braise. Meat will exude a lot of juice, and it should stay moist but not swim as it cooks. 4. Simmer slowly in oven or on stovetop, whichever is easier to monitor. 5. Allow sauce to chill overnight; excess fat will harden on surface for removal. 6. Leftovers are good for several days and freeze well.

2–2¼ lbs. trimmed boneless beef chuck (buy 3 lb.)

2 oz. (½ cup) butcher-shop bacon, cut in dice

8 oz. (1½ cups) onion, peeled and chopped

1 medium carrot, peeled and diced

1 large rib celery, trimmed and diced

3 cloves garlic, peeled and minced

1 tablespoon tomato paste

12 fl. oz. (½ bottle) (1½ cups) dry red wine

6–12 fl. oz. (¾–1½ cups) beef or chicken stock

1 bay leaf

2 full sprigs thyme (or ½ teaspoon dry)

2 sprigs parsley

scant ¼ teaspoon crushed red pepper (optional)

salt and freshly ground pepper

½ lb. (3 cups) mushrooms, sliced

walnut-sized lump roux (p. 11)

chopped fresh parsley

A note on meat: Only chuck will result in succulently tender, slowly cooked beef. A leaner cut from the hind will finish dry and crumbly. Chuck in a typical supermarket comes with a lot of fat. Figure at least ¼–⅓ trim when purchasing meat. Each pound of trimmed beef will serve 2 generously or 3 sensibly.

1. Trim meat of excess fat, cut into 2-inch chunks. Discard fat; save sinewy bits to freeze for stock. Season generously with salt and freshly ground black pepper. Place in bowl, refrigerate uncovered overnight, or leave at room temperature 1 hour.

2. Render fat from bacon in heavy frying pan over moderate heat; if lean, add a little olive oil. Remove golden bacon cubes with slotted spoon; pour rendered fat into cup.

3. Film frying pan with 1 tablespoon bacon dripping; brown beef in batches in hot skillet. As meat browns, remove with tongs to heavy ovenproof casserole (enameled cast-iron is ideal). When all meat has been browned, discard fat from frying pan.

4. Reduce heat and film frying pan with 1 tablespoon bacon fat. Add chopped onion, carrot, and celery (this mirepoix mixture should equal 3 cups.) Cover with butter papers and sweat until tender and slightly browned. Sweating vegetables will dissolve any browned bits left in skillet. Add garlic and tomato paste. Stir and sauté until garlic is fragrant.

5. Add wine; simmer a few minutes before pouring mixture over beef. Add ¾ cup stock to skillet, warm to deglaze, and add to casserole. Meat should only be ¾ covered with liquid. Sprinkle over red pepper, add bay leaf, thyme, parsley, more salt and pepper. Cover and braise slowly over very low heat on stovetop or in 325°F oven for 2–3 hours or until meat is fork-tender but not falling apart.
   Note: If beef came with bone, include bone in braise for added flavor and gelatin.

6. When meat is fully cooked, remove from heat. Uncover and cool to room temperature. Lift out bay leaf, thyme branches, and parsley. Use slotted spoon to remove chunks of meat. Store meat in 1 bowl and cooking liquid in another bowl. When fully cool, wrap and refrigerate overnight.

7. The next day lift any hardened fat from top of jelled liquid. Melt sauce to a simmer in braising casserole. Measure sauce; there should be 4 cups liquid with seasoning vegetables. Add stock if necessary to bring up amount. Bring to a simmer and grate over lump of hardened roux, or whisk in finely crumbled soft roux, and cook, stirring, to a thin, intensely flavored sauce. At this point sauce may be strained, or vegetables may be left intact. If you prefer a soup-like sauce, omit roux.

8. Clean, slice and sauté mushrooms in 2 batches, using remaining bacon fat, olive oil, or butter. Add mushrooms and meat chunks to sauce. Simmer to combine flavors, taste for seasonings. Serve with reserved bacon and chopped fresh parsley. Enough for 5 or 6.

Note: Bacon may be omitted; use olive oil for browning meat and mirepoix.

Serve with boiled new potatoes or mashed potatoes, green beans, and glazed carrots.

PARENTS' WEEKEND

Parents' Weekend descended out of the blue. As a resident on the outskirts of the college community and a non-observer of athletic events, the crush of Parents' Weekend had passed me by before I opened Mary Jo's.

One Saturday that first October, a stream of ring-clicking mothers dipped in, buying out our stash of cookies, scones, breads, soups, salads, and lasagna. It was midday, and the shelves were bare. Next year we'd be prepared.

Though we could not yet serve wine, surely the hordes in town would welcome some extra seats for dinner. We advertised, counted reservations, and cooked. Naively, we didn't know people reserve at several places and then choose. With 20 no-shows and too many leftovers, the next year we took cash, non-refundable deposits and packed the house.

For the first ten Parents' Weekends, we experimented until I zeroed in on a plan that worked so well we stoked it back into gear each time the annual event rolled around. We offered Roasted Garlic Potato or Butternut Squash Soup, Beef Bourguignon, Chicken Breast Velouté, and Spinach Lasagna. We served Apple Crumble, Carrot Cake, and Chocolate Meringue for dessert. On the actual day of the dinner, we were left to prep salad, veg, spuds, apples, and bake the zag. What a plan!

Pistachio And Currant Stuffed Chicken Breasts With Moroccan Tomato Sauce

Pretty enough for holidays with green pistachios and a bright tomato sauce alluringly scented with ginger and preserved lemon.

I recommend cooking chicken breasts on the bone. Flavor is superior, chicken is moister, and nutritional content is higher because bones add calcium. When preparing stuffed breasts, the bones may be removed after cooking and used to make a light stock.

6 medium bone-in chicken breasts (about 3 lbs.)
salt and freshly ground pepper
1 oz. (½ cup) soft breadcrumbs*
2 tablespoons chopped sun-dried tomato
2 tablespoons currants
3 tablespoons chopped unsalted pistachio nuts (or almonds)
½ small onion, diced and cooked until soft in 1 tablespoon butter
2 tablespoons chopped parsley or fresh mint

* To prepare soft breadcrumbs: Remove all crust from chunk of French, Italian or basic white bread. Cut bread into small dice. Turn on blender or processor and drop bread cubes through the feed opening as they whiz to a fluffy mass. Extra crumbs may be frozen for later use.

1. Trim and season chicken breasts. Refrigerate overnight or 30 minutes at room temperature. When ready to stuff, make a long deep slit on wing side of breast to form a pocket. Scrub hands.

2. Combine breadcrumbs, tomato, currants, pistachios, cooked (cooled) onion, and parsley for stuffing. Season with salt and pepper. If stuffing seems dry, add a tablespoon melted butter, cream, or milk. Divide into 6 lumps. Ease a lump of stuffing into pocket of each chicken breast; push it out and down evenly. Press edges together.

3. To cook chicken, first brown breasts in hot frying pan filmed with olive oil. If skillet is large and ovenproof, turn breasts skin side up and place frying pan directly in preheated 350°F oven. Or place browned breasts on small sheet pan. Bake 15 minutes, or to 140°F on instant-read thermometer. Cool chicken slightly. When warm enough to handle, pull off top skin. Gently lift stuffed, cooked breast off bone, easing your fingers underneath, pulling meat away from breast and rib bones. Cool and refrigerate if not using within an hour.

4. To serve, heat cooked boneless stuffed breasts in a covered shallow sauté pan with prepared sauce. Simmer just until hot.

Note: At home you may prefer to serve chicken on the bone. Browned, stuffed chicken breasts may be baked uncovered on top of 1-inch Moroccan Tomato Sauce for 15–20 minutes until nicely golden and cooked through. Take care not to overcook chicken breasts, which will dry out if allowed to cook beyond an internal temperature of 145°F.

Moroccan Tomato Sauce

Looks like basic tomato sauce, but has exotic flavors.

12 oz. (1 very large) onion, cut into small dice
2 fl. oz. (¼ cup) olive oil
1½ oz. (⅓ cup) fresh ginger, peeled and sliced
3–4 cloves garlic, peeled and sliced
½ teaspoon sliced fresh chili or ¼ teaspoon crushed dry red chili
¼ teaspoon ground cardamom
¼ teaspoon ground clove
1½ teaspoons ground coriander
½ teaspoon turmeric
1 teaspoon paprika
pinch cayenne (optional)
freshly ground black pepper
1 28 oz. can peeled Italian tomatoes, coarsely chopped including juice or
   2 lbs. fresh tomatoes, peeled, seeded, and diced
large sprig fresh thyme or ½ teaspoon dry thyme
¾ whole preserved lemon,* rind only, rinsed and diced (about 6 tablespoons)
fresh lemon juice and salt to taste

1. In deep sauté pan, heat oil, add onions, cover with butter papers, and sweat until onions have reduced and softened. Remove paper, increase heat, and sauté until onions are golden brown.

2. Meanwhile, grind ginger, garlic, and chili to paste in a mortar with ½ teaspoon salt or in blender, adding 2–3 tablespoons water. Combine all dry spices in small cup.

3. When onions are brown, add ginger paste, stirring constantly until garlic smells cooked. Sprinkle over dry spices and stir until fragrant. Add diced tomatoes, thyme, and bring to simmer. Add preserved lemon. Cover and cook gently at least 30 minutes. Thin with water if sauce is too thick. Add fresh lemon juice and salt to taste.

* Make *preserved lemons* at least once a year when you have a lemon surplus. Scrub and dry 3–5 lemons. Have ready a clean glass pint or quart jar and 6–12 tablespoons kosher salt. Place tablespoon of salt in jar. Cut lemons in quarters lengthwise. Place lemon pieces in jar, adding generous sprinkling of salt with each piece. Push lemons in tightly together forcing juice to run. When lemons have been added alternately with salt, there should be enough juice forced out to cover tops. Otherwise, add freshly squeezed lemon juice, making sure to leave ½-inch space at top. Cover jar first with double layer of plastic wrap, then screw on lid.

Leave jar at room temperature for 4 or 5 days, turning it upside down each day to dissolve salt. Lemons may be left at room temperature or stored in refrigerator. They will be fully softened and ready to use in a month and will keep for over a year in fridge. Preserved lemons are essential in North African dishes, enliven many salads, and add zest to sauces.

Bacon And Cheddar Stuffed Chicken Breasts In Mustard Velouté

Created for a St. Paddy's week menu, this became a cool weather standby. Served with a light mustard velouté, these chicken breasts pair nicely with scallion champ and buttered cabbage.

6 medium bone-in chicken breasts (3 lbs.) (p. 116)

2 oz. (½ cup) smoky bacon or well-flavored ham, diced

1 teaspoon olive oil

2 oz. (½ cup) finely chopped onion

1 clove garlic, minced

2 oz. (½ cup) aged white Cheddar cheese cut in ¼-inch dice

1 oz. (½ cup) soft breadcrumbs (p. 116)

1 or 2 tablespoons cream, stock, or milk

1 tablespoon chopped parsley

1 teaspoon chopped fresh sage (¼ teaspoon dry)

salt and freshly ground black pepper

1. To prepare chicken breasts: see p. 116.

2. Prepare stuffing: Sauté bacon with olive oil until all fat is rendered and bacon is golden. Remove bacon, and to remaining rendered fat add onion. Reduce heat, cover with butter papers, and sweat until softened, adding garlic during last few minutes of cooking. In bowl combine bacon, onion, diced cheese, breadcrumbs, parsley, sage, and freshly ground pepper. Moisten stuffing with cream or stock. Season with salt if needed. Divide mixture into 6 lumps. Push 1 mound cooled stuffing evenly into each prepared chicken breast; press edges together.

3. To cook chicken breasts: see p. 117.

Note: If you prefer to omit bacon, increase olive oil to one tablespoon and increase cheese to 3 oz. Proceed as directed.

4. Heat cooked de-boned chicken breasts in covered shallow saucepan or skillet with Mustard Velouté and serve surrounded with sauce.

MUSTARD VELOUTÉ

A French-style light cream sauce that we used mainly with chicken. Vary the flavor with lemon or mushrooms.

2 oz. (½ cup) minced onion

1 tablespoon butter or olive oil

1 clove garlic, finely chopped

2 fl. oz. (¼ cup) dry white wine (optional)

24 fl. oz. (3 cups) well-flavored, fat-free chicken stock*

¾ oz. (walnut-size lump) roux (p. 11)

2 fl. oz. (¼ cup) heavy cream

1 teaspoon finely chopped fresh tarragon (½ teaspoon dry)

2–3 teaspoons Dijon or grainy mustard (optional)

few drops fresh lemon juice

salt and freshly ground white pepper

* Sauce-quality stock must have a good amount of gelatin and flavor. It's best to make your own stock to get this result; I've never found it in a can. See Basic Chicken Stock (p. 3), Poached Chicken for Salad (p. 41)

1. Sweat onion covered with butter papers in oil or butter in medium saucepan over low heat until very soft, but not colored. Add garlic, cook briefly. Add wine and bubble up. Add stock and boil gently until ⅓ reduced.

2. Grate or crumble in roux whisking to smooth, lightly thickened sauce. (Sauce will seem thin but will coat back of spoon and will thicken more.) Simmer gently, uncovered 10–15 minutes. Add cream, tarragon, mustard, lemon juice, salt and pepper to taste. Simmer to combine flavors. There should be about 2 cups of royally flavored sauce. This sauce may be used straightaway or cooled, chilled, and refrigerated for 4–5 days, or frozen.

Note: To make *Mushroom Sauce*, reduce mustard to ½ teaspoon and add 8 oz. sliced, sautéed mushrooms. For *Lemon Velouté*, reduce mustard by ½ and add finely diced, rinsed rind ½ preserved lemon (p. 119), plus grated rind and juice of ½ fresh lemon. Garnish with fresh basil ribbons or parsley.

LEMON STUFFED CHICKEN BREASTS IN LEMON VELOUTÉ

Both fresh and preserved lemon add special zest. Lemon's always a hit.

6 medium bone-in chicken breasts (3 lbs.) (p. 116)
2 oz. finely chopped onion (½ small)
1 clove minced garlic
1 tablespoon butter or olive oil
1 oz. fresh breadcrumbs (½ cup) (p. 116)
½ preserved lemon (p. 119)
grated rind and juice of one small or ½ medium fresh lemon
1 tablespoon cream if needed
chopped fresh parsley and basil or mint
salt and freshly ground pepper

1. Gently sweat onion and garlic in butter until softened. Scoop out and discard the center of preserved lemon; rinse rind and cut into small dice.

Mix all ingredients together; moisten with 2 tablespoons lemon juice and cream if needed; season with salt and pepper. Use to stuff 6 chicken breasts.

2. Follow procedure for stuffing and cooking chicken breasts (p. 116–117). Serve with Lemon Velouté (p. 121).

Pecan Stuffed Chicken Breasts With Mushroom Sauce

1. Follow stuffing recipe under Lemon Stuffed Chicken Breasts (p. 122) omitting preserved and fresh lemon. Add 2 oz. (½ cup) chopped fresh pecans. Use cream to moisten crumbs. Season with fresh or dry tarragon or marjoram.

2. Follow procedure for stuffing and cooking chicken breasts (p. 116–117). Serve with Mushroom Sauce (p. 121).

The Customer Is Not Always Right

One Saturday night we were booked solid. Enter: a man in a flame-red Izod polo. He had a reservation for four, but curtly stated there would only be three: Dad, college-age son, and Dad's mom. That seemed the scene for the evening: parents and students, few wine sales. Six tables in and no wine or drinks. Not only would there be less for the till and gratuities, but folks would be cranky and impatient.

Finally, a wine sale came up: a half-bottle of Turnbull Cab. Hooray, it was for the Izod guy's party of three! Two roast pork stuffed with apples, and one grilled salmon. I made the plates extra-nice with soft mounds of polenta under the juicy pork, with a mustard-tinged Sauce Robert. The salmon glistened with fresh herb Salsa Verde while duPuy lentils brunoise oozed from underneath. Buttered sugar snaps, zucchini petals, and braised carrots wreathed each of the plates. The mains were whisked to the dining room.

My waitress, Jenn, rushed to my side at the stove. Anxiety in her eyes, she told me Mr. Izod guy wanted one entire prix fixe removed from his bill. Jenn had checked with them shortly after they were served and received no complaint. Two plates had been totally cleaned, but grandma had eaten only half her dinner. I approached the table and asked what was the matter. Dad declared his mother didn't "like" her dish. The embarrassed mother said she simply wasn't feeling well. I assured her the pork was from the best

Cincinnati butcher. I knew it was properly cooked, and everyone else had found it excellent. I suggested a packaged takeout meal she could enjoy the next day. Returning to the kitchen, I carefully placed fresh slices of pork and vegetables, plus a cup of sauce, into a to-go container, hoping to solve the dilemma.

They clean-plated two strawberry bread puddings and a lemon-raspberry meringue with coffees all around. The Izod guy spoke rudely to Jenn when his credit card wouldn't process. We each tried it three times. She was frightened; I, too, was shaking, but I returned to his table, reported the malfunction, and asked if he had another card. After rifling through a walletful of credit cards, he handed me one with another person's name; this card went through.

Grandma and son had gone outside, but — his face pinched with rage — dad remained, scribbling on the back of the credit card slip how he felt "fleeced" for having to pay for his mother's dinner and how he would send a storm of scathing e-mails that would ruin my business. He bolted out to his Lexus leaving the to-go package on the table. I wished for tougher skin. For weeks after this incident, as I locked the shop door and walked out alone into the night, I feared he might be hiding in the bushes.

WINE BRAISED DUCK LEGS

Duck is always elegant. Dealing with a whole duck means lots of fat to render. A 6-pound whole Long Island duck, which is the common breed we see, will give only 1 pound of cooked meat. The remainder is fat, skin, and bones. Duck fat is delicious to use in cooking, but most cooks today don't want to deal with it. If a roast duck presents too much fat and last-minute mess, braised duck legs are an ideal alternative. They offer the succulence of duck, ease of advance preparation, minimum fat, and less expense.

A bubbling casserole of braised duck, along with soft polenta and glazed carrots, makes an ideal main course for a winter holiday meal.

2½–3 lbs. (4 pieces) duck legs and thighs
1½ teaspoons salt
freshly ground pepper
¼ teaspoon allspice
¼ teaspoon Chinese five-spice powder (or pinch each cloves and cinnamon)
8 oz. (1 large) peeled, chopped onion
2 medium, peeled, diced carrots
1 large rib celery, trimmed and diced
4 cloves garlic, peeled and minced
pinch crushed red pepper or fresh chili
2 sprigs fresh thyme or ½ teaspoon dry thyme
1 bay leaf
1 tablespoon tomato paste
6 fl. oz. (¾ cup) red wine
6 fl. oz. (¾ cup) duck, chicken, or beef stock
½ lb. (3 cups sliced) mushrooms
2 tablespoons duck fat or butter
small lump of roux (p. 11) (optional)

1. Trim excess fat from duck legs and render in small heavy saucepan or skillet over low heat. Save at least ¼ cup. Sever tendon at duck knee by cutting through fat line at midpoint between drumstick and thigh on inside of duck leg. (This will allow duck legs to lie flat while browning rather than springing upward. Remember this trick for chicken legs with thighs as well.) Combine salt, pepper, allspice, five-spice powder, and rub seasoning mixture evenly over

duck legs. Place in bowl, cover, and refrigerate overnight or let stand at room temperature an hour.

2. In a heavy skillet, heat 1 tablespoon duck fat, and brown seasoned legs on both sides. Remove legs to an ovenproof casserole and pour off fat from pan. Film frying pan with fresh fat and add onion, carrot, celery. Cover with butter papers, reduce heat, and sweat vegetables until tender.

3. Remove papers; add garlic, red pepper, thyme, and tomato paste. Sauté a few more minutes. Stir in wine, stock, and bring to simmer. Scrape up any bits sticking to bottom of pan. Add bay leaf and pour over browned duck legs. Cover and bake in 325°F oven or braise on stovetop for 1–1½ hours or until duck is tender, but not falling apart. Slice and sauté mushrooms in duck fat or butter.

4. When duck is tender, remove legs from casserole. Sauce may be used as is or thickened slightly with roux. To thicken, bring sauce to slow bubble and grate a half-walnut-sized lump roux over simmering sauce. Stir with wooden spoon and cook until slightly thickened. Add sautéed mushrooms and taste for seasoning, adding more salt and pepper if necessary. Return duck legs to prepared sauce. Serves 4.

Note: This dish is even better the next day. Cool to room temperature, cover, and refrigerate overnight. Allow duck to come to room temperature and reheat slowly. Braised duck legs and sauce may be packaged and frozen.

This recipe, designed for home use, keeps vegetables as part of the finished sauce. In the restaurant where we cooked duck legs in quantity, we always presented braised duck with a reduction sauce. To make this type of sauce, remove duck legs when tender. Add more stock to remaining vegetable-laced juices. Allow to simmer for at least ½ hour. Strain and thicken with roux to desired consistency. Add mushrooms before serving.

Coq Au Vin

Follow basic recipe for Wine Braised Duck Legs using either 3½ lb. whole chicken cut in 8 pieces or 4 large leg/thigh sections chicken. Omit allspice and five-spice from initial seasoning. Render fat from 2 oz. diced bacon (scant ½ cup) and use 1 tablespoon bacon fat for browning chicken. Remove browning fat from skillet and use another tablespoon bacon fat for sweating vegetables. Proceed with step 2 in duck recipe (p. 126).

If using a whole chicken, braise all chicken pieces in wine mixture 20–25 minutes. Remove breast sections and continue to cook remaining chicken 20–25 minutes longer. Proceed with Wine Braised Duck Legs recipe and sprinkle bacon bits over finished dish.

BRINE CURED PORK LOIN WITH CIDER CREAM SAUCE

No other roast welcomes the harvest time of year like this combination of aromatic pork with a silken cider sauce. Serve the pork with soft polenta or mashed potatoes and buttered cabbage or broccoli.

Brining today's lean pork offers a sure way to present a moist pork roast. Leftovers are always welcome for sandwiches, salads, or stir-frys.

2½–3 lbs. boneless pork loin*
4 oz. (½ cup) kosher salt
2½ oz. (6 tablespoons) brown or white sugar
2 bay leaves
10 peppercorns
2 whole cloves
6 allspice berries
2 teaspoons dry thyme
½–1 teaspoon dry crushed red chili
3 cloves garlic
1½–2 quarts water

1. Prepare brine: Dissolve kosher salt and sugar in 1-quart room-temperature water in a tall plastic container or stainless steel bowl that will hold pork. In mortar, crack peppercorns, cloves, allspice berries; crush garlic. Add spices to brine along with crumbled bay leaves, dry thyme, crushed red pepper or 2 crumbled dry chilis. Add pork and enough water to submerge pork. Cover and refrigerate 2–3 days. (In a pinch, leave pork in brine at room temperature 3–4 hours.)

2. To cook pork, remove from brine and drain on baking tray for an hour before roasting. Preheat oven to 350°F. Because it is important not to overcook pork and to produce a browned outer edge, plan to sear outside of pork before placing it in oven. Heat a heavy iron frying pan on stovetop. Add film of olive oil or melted lard. Quickly brown fat side of loin over high heat. Turn roast upright, place ovenproof frying pan or roasting pan in oven, and roast pork for 40–50

minutes or until meat thermometer or instant-read thermometer registers 140°F. (Do not be tempted to cook pork longer; result will be dry and unappetizing. My inserted Taylor oven meat thermometer will often read 145°F when the Taylor instant-read only registers 140°F. I cannot explain this, but I go by the instant-read.) Remove pork from oven and allow to rest 20 minutes before carving.

3. To serve, cut pork into thin even slices. Do not be alarmed if part of pork is slightly pink. Brining causes meat to take on a ham-like quality. Pork is fully cooked to guidelines at 137°F. Accompany pork with Cider Cream Sauce and baked apples. Serves 6.

* I strongly recommend that pork be purchased from a reliable butcher who knows where and how the pork was raised. Our supermarkets are flooded with factory-farmed pork often pumped with water and salt solutions that present both health and environmental problems.

Note: In the restaurant it was easy to cure large cuts of pork in gallons of brine because we had the big fridge. At home a tall covered plastic gallon container works well. In cold weather, use your garage as a fridge. For larger pieces of pork or turkeys, double brine recipe (one doubled recipe brine is sufficient for 18 lb. turkey or 7 lb. pork loin; add more water if needed). Place brine in clean insulated picnic box with tight lid (line box with large plastic bag for easier clean-up). Add pork or turkey, making sure meat is submerged; cover and set in cold (maximum 45°F) garage for 2 days before cooking.

CIDER CREAM SAUCE

Make this sauce for roast pork or chicken when there's fresh cider in the farmers' markets. Green peppercorns add extra zest.

1 tablespoon butter
4–5 oz. (1 cup) onion, chopped
1 rib celery (¾ cup), thinly sliced
2 cloves garlic, sliced
sprig thyme or ¼ teaspoon dry thyme
8 fl. oz. (1 cup) fresh apple cider (with no preservatives)
24 fl. oz. (3 cups) chicken stock (p. 3)
½ oz. (1 tablespoon) roux (p. 11)
1–4 fl. oz. (2–8 tablespoons) cream (optional)
1 teaspoon green peppercorns (or a dab of grainy mustard)
lemon juice to taste

1. Melt butter in medium saucepan. Add onion, celery, garlic, cover with butter papers and sweat 10–15 minutes or until vegetables are limp and translucent. Add thyme, cider, stock, and bring to boil. Cook over moderate heat until liquid has reduced by half. If peppercorns are dry, soften in small cup of water.

2. Crumble roux into sauce, whisk to fully dissolve, and allow to simmer a few minutes to thicken. Run reduced sauce through a sieve, pushing down on vegetables to extract all soft bits. (For a fully smooth sauce, process in blender a few seconds.)

3. Return sauce to pan, add cream, lemon juice to taste, and salt if needed. Chop softened green peppercorns and add to finished sauce. Makes 2 cups.

French Style Roast Leg Of Lamb

Lamb is the most festive and delicate of red meats, though lamb is often misunderstood in this country. Most Americans have not had access to young, grass-fed lamb, and fewer know how to cook lamb properly. The French method of seasoning lamb with fresh garlic and rosemary, roasting until medium, and serving in thin, pink slices moistened with light lamb jus, is perfectly delicious. In the restaurant I placed slices of roast lamb over a small mound of Spiced Eggplant, Beans Bretonne, or Savory Bread dressing. Potatoes dauphinoise and fresh green beans make good partners for lamb. Before roasting lamb for the first time, make sure you have a reliable meat thermometer or an instant-read thermometer.

5–7 lb. bone-in leg of lamb with shank attached
3 cloves garlic
sprig of fresh rosemary (or dry rosemary)
1–2 tablespoons olive oil
salt and freshly ground pepper
large onion, carrot, 2 celery ribs and extra garlic cloves
24 fl. oz. (3 cups) lamb stock* or chicken stock (p. 3)
½–1 oz. (1–2 tablespoons) roux (p. 11)
fresh lemon juice to taste

1. Trim lamb of excess fat. Whether to remove pelvic (aitch) bone is debatable. Removing bone and tying sirloin end will make carving easier; however, this prime part of the joint will overcook, since it will then be narrower than leg midsection. I prefer to leave the aitchbone in, carve around it, and keep all meat medium to medium-rare.

2. Cut peeled garlic cloves into splinters and remove rosemary needles from sprig. Use small, sharp, paring knife to make deep holes in meat. Widen each hole with finger, and push sliver of garlic along with 3 rosemary needles in each hole. You will need to insert 15–20 slivers of garlic all over leg of lamb. Rub lamb with olive oil; sprinkle generously with salt and pepper. Set aside at room temperature 2 hours before roasting. (Lamb may be seasoned night before and brought to room temperature 1 hour before roasting.) Slice onion, carrot, and celery; add a few unpeeled garlic cloves. Place vegetables diagonally over base of 10-by-14-inch roasting pan.

3. Preheat oven to 425°F. Insert oven proof meat thermometer into thickest part of leg. Place seasoned lamb fat side up on bed of vegetables and roast for 20–30 minutes or until sizzling and beginning to brown. Reduce heat to 350°F and roast 30–40 minutes. Remove lamb promptly when thermometer reaches 130°F. Do not roast longer unless you plan to serve well-done lamb; temperature will rise 5–10 degrees as lamb rests for 20 minutes before carving. *To test lamb for doneness without a thermometer, insert long metal skewer into thick section. Hold in place to count of 10; remove skewer and place it just above your upper lip. If skewer is warmer than comfortable, lamb is done.*

Note: It never seems to take longer than an hour to roast a leg of lamb at these oven temperatures.

4. *To prepare sauce:* Lift lamb from roasting pan and pour off excess fat. Remove any vegetable bits that have burned. Pour in stock to soften all browned bits. Scrape cooked vegetables and stock into saucepan. Bring to low boil and simmer 5–10 minutes to intensify stock flavor. Crumble in roux, whisk to dissolve, and simmer to richly flavored sauce. Add fresh lemon juice to taste and correct seasoning with salt and pepper. Strain sauce through a sieve before serving. Set aside vegetables for stock.*

5. Although lamb is traditionally carved in slices perpendicular to bone, I recommend the French method of carving a leg of lamb in long thin slices parallel to bone. This method produces a generous platter of rippling slices with varying doneness. To carve this way: wrap a napkin around exposed shank bone and hold lamb steady. Carve in long, lengthwise slices, giving leg a quarter turn each time you get close to bone. Rare meat will be on underside of leg, while upper section which is closer to bone will be medium to well-done. Present a platter of carved lamb with fresh parsley and a bowl of delicious sauce. Enough for 8–10.

Note: Leftover roast lamb makes excellent salads. Thinly slice lean medium-rare lamb and dress with virgin olive oil, salt, pepper, finely chopped scallions, parsley. Serve with lemon wedges. Makes superb sandwich or topping for fresh green salad. Add Greek olives, crumbled sheep's milk feta, a wedged ripe tomato, and take yourself to the Mediterranean for lunch.

Lamb stock: After removing all meat from bone, bend at joints and cut into segments. (May store in freezer, along with browned vegetables.) Roast bones in hot oven next time you are baking bread. Place roasted bones and reserved vegetables in medium saucepan. Cover with water and simmer 2 hours to make stock for next roast lamb or pot of barley soup. Strain, cool, refrigerate, or degrease and freeze stock.

PAN GRILLED SALMON

Week after week I cooked salmon fillets in small, black, heavy frying pans. This stovetop method always produces good results as long as the frying pan is very hot to begin with.

2 5–6 oz. boneless salmon fillets with skin

1 teaspoon oil*

salt and freshly ground pepper

Season salmon with salt and pepper. Heat frying pan until it begins to smoke. Swirl in oil. Add salmon fillets flesh-side down, skin-side up. Cook over high heat 3 minutes. Turn fillets over, cover pan, reduce heat slightly, and cook another three minutes. Remove lid, lift pan from heat, turn fillets over, and pull off crisp skin. Serve the skinless fillets upright with one of the recommended sauces and garnishes.

Note: For those who prefer salmon medium rare, two minutes of cooking per side will be adequate. To test for doneness, insert a small metal skewer sideways into center of fish. Allow skewer to stand 10 seconds and test it for warmth above your upper lip. If the skewer is warm, salmon is almost done; if hot, it is definitely done.

Varieties of salmon are different. Atlantic salmon is usually preferred for its higher fat content and rich, moist flesh. Wild Atlantic is most desirable, yet it is expensive. Farmed Atlantic salmon varies in quality. Pacific salmon is leaner and dryer. Cook Pacific salmon the minimum time for a moist result. Any salmon that has been frozen will cook in less time than fresh salmon.

* Avoid using extra virgin olive oil, which doesn't tolerate high heat. Choose peanut oil, corn oil, or pomace olive oil for searing.

To cook salmon on a charcoal grill, prepare a glowing, hot bed of hardwood charcoal. Place seasoned salmon skin-side down on hot grill. Cover and cook 4–5 minutes or until small beads of white moisture appear on the surface and the fish tests done with a skewer (see above). There's no need to turn fillets when using a covered kettle style grill.

MELTING CREAMY LEEKS FOR GRILLED SALMON

When my sister lived near Seattle, she sent a box of gigantic organic leeks for my birthday. This recipe was the highlight of our leek adventure. We used it with grilled salmon, and it is equally welcome with chicken, pork, omelets, or baked potatoes.

> 2 large or 3 medium leeks (1 bunch, 1½ lbs.)
>
> 1½ oz. (3 tablespoons) butter
>
> ¼–½ teaspoon finely chopped green chili, seeds intact (optional)
>
> 2 cloves garlic, finely chopped
>
> 4 fl. oz. (½ cup) heavy cream or ½ cup béchamel sauce (p. 74)
>
> salt, freshly ground white pepper, and freshly grated nutmeg
>
> 1–2 teaspoons lemon juice

Leeks are lovely vegetables, inexpensive, and common in northern Europe, England and Ireland. However, they are pricey in most American supermarkets. A bunch of leeks should weigh about 1½ lbs., but there will be only 1 lb. usable for this recipe. (Coarse outer leaves and dark green tops may be used in soup stock. Cleaned and packed in a plastic bag, they can wait in the freezer until the next stockpot goes on the stove.)

1. Cleaning leeks can be a test of patience. Remove root and trim off coarse green by cutting the leek top into an upside-down V. Split leeks in half lengthwise and immerse in a basin of cold water. Allow leeks to soak a few minutes to moisten sand or dirt that often cakes inside leaves. Rub your fingers inside leaves to make sure all dirt is washed away. Shake out excess water and allow leeks to drain. Slice leeks thinly; there should be at least 6 cups sliced.

2. Melt butter in large stainless steel skillet or wide pot. Add sliced leeks, sprinkle with salt, cover with butter papers, and sweat gently for 30–45 minutes. Sprinkle chopped garlic and green chili on top of sweating leeks halfway through cooking. When leeks have reduced to 2 cups — they must be very tender — add cream or béchamel sauce and cook a few more minutes to a saucy consistency.

3. Season with freshly ground white pepper and grated nutmeg, adding more salt and a little lemon juice to lift flavor. Makes 2 generous cups of melting leeks, enough to garnish 6 portions of salmon.

Present leeks underneath or beside grilled salmon fillets. Garnish with parsley.

Note: For a thinner consistency, add extra cream, stock, or water to leeks.

Lentil Ragout And Red Wine Glaze For Salmon

This hearty combination makes salmon a welcome cold-weather dish and compatible with light red wines. Use French Puy lentils if possible and look for butcher-shop quality lean, smoky bacon.

3½ oz. (½ cup) French Puy green or brown lentils
1–2 oz. (¼–½ cup) smoky bacon, diced
1 teaspoon olive oil
2–3 oz. (½ cup) onion, peeled and cut in small dice
1 small (2 oz.) (⅓ cup) carrot, peeled and cut in small dice
1 medium rib celery (1½ oz.), cut in small dice (⅓ cup)
2 cloves garlic, finely chopped
1 teaspoon chopped fresh thyme leaves (pinch dry)
4 fl. oz. (½ cup) chicken stock (p. 3)
2 fl. oz. heavy cream (¼ cup)
almond-sized lump of cold roux (p. 11) (optional)
1 teaspoon finely chopped fresh tarragon (½ teaspoon dry)
lemon juice, salt and freshly ground pepper to taste

1. Cook lentils in 1½ cups water in covered saucepan for 15 minutes or until tender but still holding shape. Add ½ teaspoon salt and allow to stand off heat 15 minutes. (You should have a generous cup of drained, cooked lentils.)

2. Cook bacon in olive oil in medium saucepan until fat renders and bacon is light golden brown. There should be a tablespoon of rendered fat in pan. Add onion, carrot, and celery to bacon, reduce heat to moderate, cover with butter papers or waxed paper, and sweat 10–12 minutes, until vegetables are tender.

3. Remove paper, add garlic and thyme, and sauté a few more minutes. Add chicken stock and bring to simmer. Pour lentils into sieve; shake off dark cooking liquid and add lentils to seasoned stock. Simmer lentils in stock 10 minutes; add salt and pepper if needed.

4. Add heavy cream and simmer to reduce slightly. If mixture seems too thin, grate small lump of roux into saucepan (use small hand-held grater); stir and simmer until thickened slightly. Add fresh tarragon, squeeze of lemon juice, and correct seasonings, adding more salt and pepper if necessary. Makes enough ragout for 4 servings.

Note: If you prefer to omit bacon, increase olive oil to 1½ tablespoons and proceed with recipe.

This ragout may be made the day before and reheated as needed. It also freezes well. Add sautéed mushrooms to any leftovers and use as sauce for pasta. Double recipe to guarantee leftovers.

Red Wine Glaze

A very small amount of this strongly flavored glaze lifts salmon or chicken to regal heights.

½ cup fruity red wine such as Australian Shiraz or California Merlot
½ teaspoon honey
1 oz. (2 tablespoons) butter
pinch of salt

In a small heavy saucepan, reduce wine over moderate heat until there is less than a tablespoon of syrup on bottom of pan. Watch carefully so wine does not burn at edge of saucepan. Remove from heat. Add honey. Cut butter in four slices, and use a tiny whisk or a fork to blend in butter one slice at a time. Season with salt. Hold glaze in a place where it will stay lukewarm (set the saucepan in a bowl of warm water). Glaze should be the consistency of heavy syrup, and 2 teaspoons per serving will be sufficient.

To Serve Salmon with Lentil Ragout and Red Wine Glaze:
Warm lentil ragout, and make sure glaze is just liquid enough to drizzle. Pan grill salmon fillets as directed.

On each plate or on a serving platter, place generous spoonfuls of lentil ragout. Top each mound of lentils with fillet of grilled salmon. Drizzle glaze over salmon and use any extra to dot around edge of ragout. Sprinkle with chopped parsley.

BALLYMALOE SPINACH SAUCE FOR SALMON

A brilliant butter sauce with lots of tender spinach. When served with pink grilled salmon, it's a feast for all the senses. Please do not be dismayed by the cream and butter; a little goes a long way and awards flavor that can't be beat. From one of Ireland's best tables.

4 fl. oz. (½ cup) heavy cream
2 oz. (½ stick) butter
5 oz. (½ large bunch) washed spinach leaves
salt and freshly ground white pepper

1. In a small heavy saucepan, preferably enameled cast iron, bring cream to a simmer. Let cream cook slowly for 15–20 minutes, stirring occasionally until reduced by half. It should become a thick, pale-yellow mass.

2. While cream reduces, wash spinach, pull off stems, and slice leaves into ribbons. There will be 4 cups spinach leaves. Place spinach in heavy saucepan, add pinch of salt, and 1 tablespoon water. Cover and cook quickly until spinach is wilted. After cooking, spinach will have reduced to about ½ cup. Set aside spinach and any remaining liquid.

3. When cream has reduced (be careful not to let it burn), cut butter in slices, turn heat very low, and whisk butter into cream a few slices at a time. The resulting sauce should look like thin mayonnaise. Season with salt and white pepper. Stir in wilted spinach and add spinach liquid if needed. The sauce should be thin and luxuriously flavorful. Serves 3 or 4.

To serve Salmon with Ballymaloe Spinach Sauce:
Hold spinach sauce in a warm water bath by placing saucepan in a bowl of hot water. (If sauce gets too hot, it may split. It is best served warm.) Place grilled salmon fillets on serving plates or platter. Use tongs to place some creamy spinach ribbons near the side or on top of each fillet, and spoon buttery, spinach-flecked sauce around salmon. Alternatively ladle a pool of spinach sauce on plate or platter and place grilled salmon on top of sauce. Garnish with freshly ground pepper and parsley if desired.

CODDLED CABBAGE AND SHERRY VINAIGRETTE FOR GRILLED SALMON

Richly flavored cabbage beneath and a drizzle of nutty, sherry vinaigrette on top, give juicy grilled salmon a big city restaurant look. Choose Savoy cabbage if possible, though fresh green homegrown cabbage is just fine. Coddled cabbage is also excellent with pork.

1¼ lb. fresh green cabbage or 1 lb. Savoy cabbage
2 oz. (½ cup) smoky bacon, diced
3 oz. (generous ½ cup) finely chopped onion
2 cloves garlic, minced
2 fl. oz. (¼ cup) heavy cream
2 tablespoons cider vinegar
salt and pepper to taste
1 tablespoon chopped fresh dill or parsley

1. Snap off green outer cabbage leaves and wash well. Remove ribs. Roll leaves and chop into thin ribbons, or cut leaves into long wide ribbons and cut crosswise into small squares. Set aside. Cut whole cabbage in quarters lengthwise. Slice core from each wedge, and cut each quarter into thin ribbons or dice. Total amount of cut cabbage should measure 6 cups. Keep outer and inner cut cabbage separated.

2. In large saucepan or medium enameled Dutch oven, sauté bacon until it has rendered fat and is lightly browned. Lower heat; remove bacon with slotted spoon and add chopped onion to bacon fat. Gently sauté onion for 5 minutes or until almost tender. Add garlic and stir to cook briefly. Raise heat and add prepared outer leaves of cabbage. These are tougher and will need to cook longer. Stir cabbage in onion-scented bacon fat to wilt and allow to cook 3–4 minutes. Add remaining cabbage and keep heat brisk enough to wilt cabbage, but do not allow it to brown. As soon as cabbage glistens and is beginning to wilt, season with salt, add cream and 4 tablespoons water. Cover and cook 6–7 minutes or until tender. Add vinegar, stir to combine. Allow juices to bubble uncovered 2 minutes. Cover and simmer another 2 minutes to combine flavors. Check for doneness and seasoning; add finely chopped dill or parsley and reserved bacon. Use as soon as possible or spread out to cool, and reheat for serving. Makes 4 cups or enough for 6.

SHERRY VINAIGRETTE

1 small clove garlic mashed with ¼ teaspoon salt

1 tablespoon sherry vinegar

1 teaspoon medium or dry sherry (or white wine)

½ teaspoon Dijon mustard

3 tablespoons extra virgin olive oil

In a small bowl combine garlic, vinegar, and sherry. Using a fork, blend in mustard and whisk in olive oil. Hold at room temperature until ready to use. Makes 4 tablespoons.

When salmon is ready to be served, place a mound of warm coddled cabbage (a generous ½ cup) on a serving plate. Nestle grilled, skinned salmon fillet on top of cabbage. Drizzle each fillet with sherry vinaigrette. Serve with chopped fresh parsley.

SOUTH INDIAN SHRIMP CURRY

For twenty years I held onto the memory of an unforgettable shrimp curry discovered in a small upstairs Indian restaurant in Accra, Ghana. When I finally made the match, this was our favorite shrimp preparation.

2 tablespoons vegetable oil plus 2 tablespoons butter or ghee*
1 lb. (2½–3 cups) onions, peeled and thinly sliced
1–2 green chilis (cayenne or serrano)
1 oz. (7–8 cloves) garlic, peeled and sliced
2 oz. (½ cup) fresh ginger, peeled and sliced
2 teaspoons garam masala (p. 13)
1 tablespoon turmeric
1 tablespoon ground coriander
1 teaspoon ground cumin
¼ teaspoon cayenne
1 13.5 oz. can unsweetened coconut milk (Chaokoh brand)
1¼ lbs. shrimp in shells, peeled and deveined
fresh lime juice and cilantro

1. Heat butter and oil in a deep frying pan; add onions. Sauté, stirring occasionally, until totally softened and deeply golden brown. This step will take 40 minutes. Onions will reduce to a dark, soft mass on pan bottom.

2. Meanwhile, thinly slice one chili; leave one whole. Grind sliced chili, garlic, and ginger to paste with l teaspoon salt in stone mortar or grind in blender with ¼ cup water. Combine all dry spices in small cup.

3. When onions are reduced, stir in ginger paste and sauté, stirring until garlic smells cooked, at least 2 minutes (this step will take longer if there is water in ginger paste). Sprinkle in dry spices and continue stirring until mixture smells fragrant. Add whole chili. Pour in coconut milk plus 1 can of water and simmer gently for ½ hour. Remove whole chili if sauce becomes too spicy. Boil to reduce if sauce seems too thin. Correct seasoning, adding more salt if needed.

4. Shortly before serving, add shrimp and simmer 3–5 minutes or until shrimp turn color and cook through. Add lime juice to taste plus a generous handful of coarsely chopped cilantro. Serve with Rice Pilaf (p. 146) and Cucumber Raita (p. 48) Enough for 4–6.

* Indian clarified butter

Rice Pilaf

10 oz. (1½ cups) basmati rice
1 scant tablespoon butter, ghee, or vegetable oil
½ small onion finely chopped
1 teaspoon coriander seed
1 large splinter Ceylon cinnamon or small bit cinnamon stick
small pinch turmeric or powdered saffron
½ teaspoon salt
16 fl. oz. (2 cups) soaking water

1. Wash rice in cold water, changing water twice. Drain, cover with fresh water, and soak 20–30 minutes.

2. Meanwhile, melt ghee or oil in heavy saucepan with tight-fitting cover and gently sauté onion with coriander seeds, cinnamon, and turmeric or saffron. Drain rice, retaining 16 fl. oz. (2 cups) soaking water. Stir rice and salt into onion mixture. Pour in water; stir again to dissolve salt. Cover, bring to boil, and cook over low heat for 10 minutes, or until water is absorbed. Fluff with fork; place clean cloth napkin or tea towel between rice and lid to absorb moisture. Allow rice to rest covered for 10 minutes before serving. Enough for 4–6.

DINNER NOTES

VEGETABLES

Our lunch and dinner plates glistened with seasonal vegetables. Ever-present and carefully prepared, vegetables brought lightness, color, and wholesomeness into our festive dining.

Once I lived in a remote village where the only fresh vegetable I could buy for two months was cabbage. Creative necessity brought us slaws, stir frys, soups, and stews. Even now when I walk through the supermarket vegetable display in winter, I'm drawn to the cabbages. I see shipped-in green beans often pocked with brown, zucchini feeling limp at the blossom end, snow peas at astronomical prices, as well as cauliflower that is too white and broccoli bound in heavy shrink wrap.

The display of cabbages — green, napa, red, Savoy — is always inviting to the eye and the pocketbook. When I realize how much I can buy for so little, I return to the old-fashioned dishes that our grandmothers took for granted and to the health claims of the cruciferae.

One twenty-year-old waitress claimed she had never seen or tasted cooked cabbage in her life! Cabbage has been out to pasture too long; it's time to bring it back.

How To Cook Green Vegetables

On every dinner plate, we included one or two crisp green vegetables. These offerings changed with the seasons. We used the same method for each, varying the cooking time.

1. Wash vegetables and prepare for cooking:

Remove stem ends from green beans; leave tail intact.
Separate broccoli crowns from stems.
Cut cauliflower into quarters.
Slice off zucchini stems.
Remove outer leaves and quarter Brussels sprouts.
Break off tough asparagus ends.
Remove stem ends and strings from snow peas.

2. Bring a large pot of water to a boil; salt generously. Add only enough vegetables at a time to maintain boil or allow boil to return quickly. Cook each vegetable group separately. Suggested cooking times:

green beans: 4 minutes
broccoli crowns: 2 minutes, stems: 4 minutes
cauliflower: 2 minutes
small zucchini: 2 minutes, medium zucchini: 3 minutes
Brussels sprouts: 2 minutes
asparagus: 2 minutes
snow peas: 10 seconds

3. As each batch is cooked, sweep veg from boiling water with wide wire Chinese spider, big slotted spoon, or strainer. Spread cooked vegetables out on baking sheets to cool quickly. Cut cauliflower and broccoli into florets; peel stems and slice into coins; halve and diagonally slice zucchini; diagonally cut green beans and snow peas if desired.

4. When ready to serve, melt a little butter in a skillet. Add cooked room-temperature green vegetables. Toss to coat, cover to steam until heated through, and tip into serving dish.

Note: In the restaurant all our vegetables were cooked before service. For each order I used a small "veg" skillet with a cover. At one side of this skillet, I placed a spoonful of braised carrots; on the other side a handful of cut blanched green beans, broccoli, zucchini, et cetera. I added a small slice of butter and a spoonful of water. The skillet steamed a minute to heat vegetables through. The vegetables went onto the plates glistening and hot, bright green, and crisp.

Buttered Cabbage

My tribute to Ireland would not be complete without a basic recipe for cooked cabbage, an all but forgotten vegetable on our shores. It's simple, healthy, inexpensive, and almost too good to be true.

> 1–1¼ lbs. green cabbage, Savoy if possible
> 2–3 tablespoons butter
> salt
> 2–4 tablespoons water

1. Cut cabbage through the top into quarters. Cut out tough core. Slice each quarter into thin ribbons. There will be 5–6 cups.

2. Choose a large heavy pot for cooking. Bring to a boil 2 tablespoons butter with 2 tablespoons water and pinch of salt. Begin to add cabbage, ¼ at a time. Toss cabbage in hot butter and as it begins to wilt, add another ¼ cabbage. Continue until all cabbage has been added. Pour in 2 tablespoons more water if needed and cover. Cook quickly until cabbage is tender 3–5 minutes. Cabbage should still be pale green and freshly sweet. Add more salt if needed, more butter if desired. Serves 4.

Cabbage is best served straightaway; however, it may be cooked ahead, cooled, and quickly reheated.

Note: If at any time cabbage seems dry, add a little water. Savoy cabbage usually needs more liquid than regular green cabbage.

CURRIED CABBAGE AND CAULIFLOWER COOKED WITH TOMATO

Serve as a side dish with curry or prepare as a vegetarian entree to offer with lentils, rice, and yogurt.

2 tablespoons vegetable oil or 1 tablespoon butter, or ghee*
+ 1 tablespoon oil
1 teaspoon black mustard seed
½ teaspoon cumin seed
1 small onion, thinly sliced (scant cup)
¼–½ red or green chili, thinly sliced, seeds intact
1 tablespoon grated or slivered fresh ginger
½ teaspoon turmeric
2 medium tomatoes, diced (or 1 cup canned tomato)
1 medium potato, peeled and diced
½ small cabbage, sliced (2 cups)
¼–½ (2 cups) cauliflower broken into florets
salt and mango powder, lemon or lime to taste
cilantro or mint for garnish

* Indian clarified butter

1. In a large frying pan with cover, heat oil or ghee until it begins to shimmer. Add mustard and cumin seeds, cover, allow to pop, and reduce heat. Remove cover and add sliced onion and sauté until limp and golden.

Add sliced chili, ginger, turmeric; stir to cook briefly before adding tomatoes. As soon as tomatoes release liquid, add diced potato, sliced cabbage, season with salt, cover, and half-cook.

2. Mix in cauliflower, adding a little water if necessary and continue to simmer until all vegetables are tender. Season with salt and 1 teaspoon dry mango powder or lime juice to taste. Garnish with cilantro or mint. Serves 4.

This basic stir-fry and steaming method for vegetables may be used with green beans, broccoli, zucchini, Swiss chard, or other vegetable combinations.

WALTER

When I opened the shop, I knew next to nothing about financial matters: taxes, payroll, workers' comp, and so forth. My lawyer suggested I call Walter. An elderly CPA who had recently retired, Walter took me under his wing.

Invariably decked out in coat and tie, white-haired Walter strode into the kitchen every morning asking, "How's folksies?" He gathered the mail, paid the bills, and kept all the books in pencil-filled ledgers. Eager to see his "little pie shop" succeed, he kept me fiscally afloat and charged me a song. Six years later, on a morning walk, he fell and broke his hip. Gradually, he gave up his clients.

When he left, the wolves knocked at my door. A payroll provider persuaded me to let her draw checks on my bank account and proceeded to withdraw $300 for herself as a "penalty" for an unsigned form. An out-of-town accountant charged $250 for a fabricated financial statement, and an advisor convinced me I owed the Pension Guarantee Corporation $1,200 in fines; later I learned this was a result of his mismanagement. I was too overwhelmed to fight, and my legal fees would have cost more than my losses. So I dug in and learned to sort the jabberwock — as Walter's eventual replacements, Kris, Karen, and Sara, set me straight.

Glazed Carrots

Surely this is one of the best ways to cook carrots — no water needed!

1 lb. carrots, peeled and trimmed
1 tablespoon butter
pinch salt
pinch sugar (optional)

1. Choose a heavy saucepan with tightly fitting lid.

2. Cut carrots into ¼-inch slightly angled slices.

3. Place butter in saucepan; add carrots. Sprinkle with salt and optional sugar (use only if carrots lack sweetness). Cover and cook over moderately brisk heat 8–12 minutes.

4. Open; stir with rubber spatula. Carrots should be tender, juicy, glazed, and sweet. Carrots themselves exude enough liquid when cooking. Serves 4.

CORN PUDDING

When we bought summer corn in big brown bags of ten dozen ears, we cut the kernels for salads, soups, and baked trays of corn pudding in small Pyrex cups. Add this old-fashioned custard to dinners with chicken, pork, salmon or enjoy it alone with a tomato salad for lunch.

12 oz. corn cut from 3–4 large ears (2 cups)
2 eggs
6 fl. oz. cream or half-and-half (¾ cup)
½ teaspoon salt
generous grinding white pepper
generous grating nutmeg
1 tablespoon butter
1 oz. finely chopped onion (¼ cup)
1 oz. red pepper cut in small dice (¼ cup)
1 clove garlic finely chopped (optional)
⅛–¼ teaspoon finely chopped red or green fresh chili (optional)
1 tablespoon chopped parsley

1. Shuck corn and rub off silk. Using a very sharp, small knife, cut through middle of corn kernels letting them fall into a bowl. Scrape knife blade over cut cobs to squeeze out corn pulp. Do not cut kernels deeply but do scrape cobs thoroughly. Weigh or measure corn pulp and kernels.

2. In small saucepan, melt butter and sweat chopped onion, pepper, garlic, and chili over low heat until softened but not brown.

3. Whisk eggs, add cream, salt, pepper, and nutmeg. Mix in corn. Add cooked onion, pepper, garlic, and chili. Stir in parsley. Taste for seasonings.

4. Preheat oven to 350°F. Butter 6 small custard cups or 4-cup glass baking dish. Divide custard among 6 cups or pour into baking dish. Fill rectangular baking pan with ½-inch water. Place filled custard dishes in water bath and bake for 30–35 minutes or until puffed, golden and firm.

5. Serve pudding warm, spooned from baking dish or scoop individual custards from cups with rubber spatula, first loosening sides. Garnish with parsley. Serves 6.

Note: Individual corn puddings may be prepared ahead and reheated briefly in a microwave.

Mashed Potatoes

I marveled at this potato cooking method during my first stint in the Ballymaloe kitchen. In my restaurant we kept a big pot of mashed potatoes warm in a low oven and used a piping bag to form neat rosettes on each plate. When we had leftover mashed potatoes, we added them to a broth laced with onion and celery for quick potato soup or sautéed them as potato cakes for lunch.

3–4 medium russet or Idaho potatoes* (1¼–1½ lbs.)
salt
6–8 fl. oz. whole milk, half-and-half, or milk mixed with cream (¾–1 cup)
2 tablespoons butter

* For fluffy mashed potatoes, you must use floury potatoes. Choose same variety sold as baking potatoes. Red potatoes, boiling potatoes, and waxy golden potatoes are not dry enough to fluff when mashed.

1. Scrub potatoes, place in medium saucepan, add generous pinch salt, cover with water, place over moderately high heat, and boil covered for 15 minutes. Pour off most of water; return to heat and continue to cook covered for 20 minutes longer or until potatoes test tender when pierced with a toothpick. Pour off all water and return to low heat. Steam covered for 5 minutes. Meanwhile, heat milk with cream and butter in small saucepan.

2. Have ready a food mill, ricer, sieve, or potato masher. Tip hot potatoes out into bowl; cover with tea towel. Clean cooking pan with hot water; place food mill over hot cooking pan. Hold each hot potato with tea towel and quickly pull off skin with paring knife. Chunk hot potatoes into food mill. Continue peeling hot potatoes. Run tender chunks of potato through food mill, ricer, or sieve quickly — or mash in hot pan. Pour in hot milk with melted butter a little at a time, beating with wooden spoon to desired consistency. Season with salt and pepper, adding more butter if desired. Serves 4.

To make a delicious *Scallion Champ*: Add 4–5 chopped green onions (½–¾ cup) to warming milk. The finished whipped potatoes will be flecked with lovely bits of green.

Note: Boiling potatoes in their skins preserves more nutrients than boiling peeled potatoes. Also, cooked potatoes are easier to peel.

Gratin Dauphinoise

The ideal potato dish to cook alongside a roast. Always make more than needed; it's delicious the next day warmed or at room temperature with a salad for a light meal. This has always been my family's favorite potato dish.

2 lbs. Idaho or russet potatoes or 2¼ lbs. Yukon gold or white potatoes
scant tablespoon finely chopped garlic
1 teaspoon salt
generous grinding white or black pepper
8 fl. oz. whole milk (1 cup)
4 fl. oz. heavy cream (½ cup)*
1½ oz. butter (3 tablespoons)*
2 oz. grated cheese, Gruyère, or aged white Cheddar (½ cup)

1. Preheat oven to 400–425°F. Sprinkle chopped garlic, salt, and pepper in a 2-quart low oval or rectangular baking dish. Add milk, cream, and sliced butter. Place in oven to heat.

2. Peel and cut potatoes into $^1/_8$-inch slices. (If necessary, this may be done 30 minutes ahead and potatoes may be covered with cold water.)

3. Remove hot baking dish with simmering milk from oven. Evenly strew in sliced potatoes. Sprinkle with grated cheese. Return to oven.

4. Bake 25–40 minutes. The top should be golden brown and potatoes fork-tender. If potatoes seem dry, add 2 tablespoons water and allow to rest a few minutes. Serves 6.

* If you choose to omit cream, increase milk to 1½ cups and butter to 2 oz. or 4 tablespoons.

SOFT POLENTA

This polenta is good enough to eat alone and complements a host of meats, fish, or vegetarian dishes. Try it with braised beef, chicken, salmon, or buttered cabbage. Polenta is a welcome change from rice and potatoes.

32 fl. oz. water (4 cups)
1 teaspoon finely chopped garlic
1 teaspoon chopped fresh rosemary (optional)
5 oz. coarse or medium polenta (1 scant cup)
1 teaspoon salt
2 tablespoons butter
1 oz. grated Parmesan cheese (¼ cup packed) (optional)

1. Choose a wide heavy pot, at least 2½ quarts. Bring water to boil with garlic and rosemary. Gradually pour in polenta, stirring constantly with a wide whisk or wooden spoon. Add salt and cook over moderate heat a few minutes until it thickens into a thin porridge. Reduce heat to low and allow polenta to cook slowly for 30–40 minutes, stirring from time to time. Polenta should reach consistency of mashed potatoes. Taste occasionally to see if grains are cooked and feel fully softened. If polenta becomes too thick, losing its creamy consistency, add a little water and continue to cook.

2. When polenta is cooked, add butter, Parmesan cheese, and salt to taste.

3. Pour polenta into a warm serving bowl when ready to use, or hold polenta covered in a warm oven. Serves 4–6.

Note: If you have cooked extra polenta, before serving, spoon hot excess into loaf pan rinsed with cold water and allow polenta to cool. Refrigerate and unmold onto cutting board. Slice and sauté in butter or olive oil until brown on both sides for crispy polenta leftovers.

Tomatoes Provençal

Nothing sings of summer in the South of France like Tomatoes Provençal. I first tasted these in Aix where an elderly American tourist shared them from her table. Again, we have the harmonious quartet of tomatoes, olive oil, garlic, and bread. Serve these tomatoes warm with a roast or at room temperature with salads and picnic food. Leftovers are excellent in sandwiches, quiche, or omelets.

> 4 ripe summer tomatoes each 2½ inches wide (1¼ lbs.)
> salt
> 1 oz. soft breadcrumbs (p. 116) (½ cup packed)
> 1 oz. finely chopped parsley (½ cup packed)
> 2 medium cloves garlic, mashed to paste with ¼ teaspoon salt
> freshly ground pepper
> 4 tablespoons olive oil

1. Do not core tomatoes. Cut in half at equator. Use your finger to scoop out seedy bits. Sprinkle tomato halves with salt; turn cut sides down on a plate and let drain 30 minutes.

2. Combine breadcrumbs, parsley, mashed garlic, and a little salt, working mixture together with your fingertips.

3. Preheat oven to 350°F (or use whatever temperature you have going for something else). Place drained tomato halves, cut side up, around 9-inch glass pie plate or other flat baking dish. Cover tops of tomatoes with parsley/crumb mixture. Use all crumbs over tomato halves. Drizzle 4 full tablespoons olive oil over crumb-topped tomatoes, and grind over black pepper. Bake 30–40 minutes or until crumbs have browned and tomatoes are tender. Spoon any olive oil left in baking dish over tomatoes. Serves 4.

Whenever I served rack or leg of lamb, I added a spoonful of Spiced Eggplant, Beans Bretonne, or Savory Greek Dressing tucked under the sliced medium roast lamb. This complemented the meat and boosted the look of the presentation without taking the meat portion beyond the cost allowed. Because we always kept our dinner prices moderate, these inexpensive garnishes not only beefed out the meat servings but kept our main courses interesting and light.

SPICED EGGPLANT

This braised eggplant is lifted with Indian spices, vinegar and brown sugar.

1 eggplant 1–1¼ lbs.
4 tablespoons olive or vegetable oil
1 medium onion, peeled and chopped (1 generous cup)
2 garlic cloves, peeled and sliced
½ green or red fresh chili, sliced (or pinch dry chili)
1 tablespoon finely grated peeled fresh ginger
1 teaspoon ground coriander
½ teaspoon ground cumin
½ teaspoon ground turmeric
¼ teaspoon garam masala (p. 13)
1 14½ oz. can tomatoes chopped, juice included or 1¼ lbs. summer
   tomatoes, peeled, seeded (juice retained) and chunked (p. 19)
1 tablespoon wine vinegar
1 rounded teaspoon brown sugar
salt to taste
finely chopped fresh mint, cilantro, or parsley

1. Choose an eggplant that has dark, almost black skin and a fresh-looking green top. To remove excess water: Cut eggplant into ½-inch slices and cut slices into ½-inch dice. Mix 1 tablespoon salt with 1 quart cold water in deep plastic container or bowl. Add diced eggplant; cover with small plate; and weight down with cup of water set on plate. Leave eggplant in salt water for at least ½ hour. Drain; shake eggplant dry. [The salt solution will draw excess moisture and any bitterness from eggplant. Some recipes recommend sprinkling eggplant with salt to drain; however, a salt water bath prevents eggplant from discoloring or becoming too salty.]

2. In a deep sauté pan or stewing pot, heat oil and add chopped onion. Sauté gently until onion is deep golden brown. Meanwhile, combine garlic, chili, and ginger in mortar; add ½ teaspoon salt and pound to a paste. Or mash garlic on cutting board and combine with finely chopped chili and grated ginger. Measure dry spices into small cup.

3. When onions are golden, add ginger paste and stir constantly until garlic and ginger smell cooked. Add dry spices and stir until fragrant. Add eggplant and mix into spiced onions. Sauté briefly, but do not let spice paste burn. Add tomatoes, scrape up bits on pan bottom, and season with extra salt if needed. Cover and reduce heat to simmer. Continue to cook eggplant 30–45 minutes or until tender. Uncover and reduce liquid if necessary. Add vinegar, brown sugar and simmer a few more minutes to combine flavors. Taste for seasonings, adding chopped herbs when serving. Makes 4 cups.

Note: Spiced eggplant is also delicious at room temperature as part of a salad plate with a dollop of homemade plain yogurt, or as a sandwich filling.

BEANS BRETONNE: WHITE BEANS WITH HERBS AND TOMATO

The classic Haricots Bretonne, always welcome with roast lamb or pork. Omit the bacon for a vegetarian mainstay.

1 lb. great Northern dry white beans

1 ham hock, 3 slices bacon, or 1 tablespoon olive oil

1 bay leaf

2 whole cloves garlic

1 dry small red chili (optional)

8 oz. (2 cups) onion, peeled and diced

2 tablespoons olive oil

2 cloves garlic, finely chopped

2 teaspoons chopped fresh thyme or ½ teaspoon dry

a few slices fresh chili or pinch crushed red pepper (optional)

1 14½-oz. can tomatoes, or 1 lb. fresh ripe tomatoes in season, peeled, seeded, and diced (p. 19)

salt and freshly ground pepper

chopped fresh parsley

1. Rinse dry beans; cover with water and allow to soak overnight. Drain beans, cover with two quarts fresh water, add ham hock, bacon, or 1 tablespoon oil, bay leaf, whole garlic, and whole chili. Cover, bring to simmer and cook over low heat 2–3 hours or until beans are buttery tender. (Beans may be cooked in a tightly covered ovenproof casserole in a moderate oven, if oven is on for something else.) Remove hock or bacon, bay leaf, garlic, and chili. Season with salt. (Dice hock meat and save.)

2. In a 3-quart saucepan, gently sauté onion in 2 tablespoons olive oil for l5 minutes or until tender but not brown. Add chopped garlic, thyme, and chili; sauté until garlic smells cooked. Add chopped tomato and cook until thickened.

3. If there is over a quart of liquid in beans, drain ¾ off and add to tomato mixture. Reduce by ½. Gently mix in cooked beans and simmer with tomato base for 30 minutes. Allow mixture to thicken to desired consistency. Taste for seasonings, adding more salt and pepper as needed. Garnish with parsley. Makes 2 quarts.

Note: This dish will have more flavor if cooled, refrigerated overnight, and reheated the next day. It's also delicious at room temperature with yogurt, a drizzle of olive oil, and green salad for lunch.

Savory Greek Dressing

This bread dressing may be used as a side dish with any roast, or as a baked casserole on its own.

4 tablespoons olive oil

2 tablespoons butter

4 oz. (2 cups) mushrooms sliced

1 medium onion (6 oz.), chopped (1 generous cup)

2 oz. (1 cup) thinly sliced fennel or celery

1–2 cloves garlic, chopped

½ cup mixed chopped fresh herbs (parsley, basil, thyme, sage, oregano, mint, rosemary—use more mild herbs, less strong herbs) or chopped fresh parsley plus ½ teaspoon each dry thyme, sage, oregano

1–2 anchovy fillets, chopped (optional)

2–3 oz. (½ cup) feta cheese, crumbled

10 Kalamata olives, pitted and sliced (or other olives)

8 oz. (5 cups) French or sourdough bread, cubed

salt and pepper

4–6 fl. oz. (½–¾ cup) chicken stock, milk, or cream

1 oz. (¼ cup) grated white Cheddar

1. Sauté mushrooms in 1 tablespoon olive oil and 1 tablespoon butter. Scrape into a bowl.

2. Add remaining butter and 1 tablespoon oil to skillet and gently sauté onion and celery until tender. Add garlic and cook until fragrant. Combine onions and mushrooms.

3. Add chopped herbs, anchovy, feta, olives and toss with cubed bread. Season with salt and pepper; moisten with chicken stock, milk or cream.

4. Smear a 2-quart rectangular glass baking dish with olive oil and scrape in dressing, leveling evenly. Sprinkle with grated cheese and drizzle with last tablespoon olive oil.

5. Bake dressing alongside whatever roast is going in the oven, or bake at 350°F for 30–40 minutes until top is crispy and lightly browned. Serves 6–8.

VEGETABLE NOTES

FINGER FOODS

*R*equests for party food came on the busiest weekends. We soon learned fiddly bits took far too much time, so we relied on popular preparations cut in small pieces or fancy pickups that could be put together quickly.

Smoked Salmon Canapés

The classic canapé for smoked salmon—and the way to extend it the furthest.

freshly baked Ballymaloe Brown Yeast Bread (p. 94) cooled and thinly sliced
unsalted butter, softened
sliced smoked salmon
finely chopped green onion and parsley
freshly ground black pepper
lemon wedges*

Spread bread slices lightly with butter. Top with salmon, covering slice entirely. Sprinkle with green onion; grind over fresh pepper. Cut each slice in half or quarters diagonally to form large or small triangles. Arrange triangles slightly overlapping on platter. Sprinkle with chopped parsley; garnish with lemon wedges.

* To cut lemons into small, easy-to-squeeze wedges: Cut lemon in half at the equator (midsection). Wedge each half into 4 or 5 sections. These small wedges are much easier to squeeze than wedges cut from the whole length of the lemon.

Finger Sandwiches

Easy to eat, simple to prepare. These tiny sandwiches sustained countless receptions. The following recipe will make 20 or more 3½-by-4-inch sandwiches with Ballymaloe Brown Yeast Bread (p. 94). Cut into triangles, the 20 sandwiches will make 80 tea or cocktail bits.

1 lb. cream cheese, softened
¼ lb. soft butter (1 stick)
1 large or 2 small cloves garlic mashed to a paste with a little salt
2 oz. (¾–1 cup) finely chopped green onion, including tops (generous half a bunch)
1 oz. (½ cup) finely chopped parsley
fresh dill or tarragon finely chopped to taste or generous pinch dry herbs
salt and freshly ground pepper to taste

1. Cream butter and cheese together until smooth. Beat in garlic paste. Mix in green onion, parsley, and chopped herbs. Season with salt and pepper.

2. Lay out several slices of bread. Top each with generous scoop of filling (use ice-cream scoop). Spread filling evenly over bread, top with another slice, press firmly, and even edges with spreading knife. Cover sandwiches and chill until firm.

3. When ready to serve, shave off side crusts with sharp knife, and cut each sandwich twice diagonally, making 4 triangles. Arrange triangles on tray, center points upward. Arrange sandwiches snugly together to keep them moist and garnish with sprigs of parsley, mint, and small fresh edible flowers.

A Few Variations On Basic Filling.
Use Each Separately.

- 4 oz. softened blue cheese beaten into cream cheese and butter
- 3 oz. (1 cup) chopped pecans or chopped roasted almonds
- sliced black olives
- softened finely chopped sun-dried tomato plus chopped fresh basil
- minced peeled roasted red pepper

Quiche In Squares

Mary Jo's could never make enough quiche. We often baked big ones in cookie sheets and cut them in squares for finger food. Spinach quiche became the standard. It was easy to cut and always popular.

1 full recipe quiche pastry (p. 56)

5 cup quiche filling (1¼ recipe quiche filling, p. 58)

2 lbs. frozen chopped spinach, thawed

1⅓ cup sautéed onion with garlic (p. 59)

fresh dill or dry dill weed

12 oz. (3 cups) grated Swiss cheese or mixture of Swiss and white Cheddar

grated fresh nutmeg

salt and freshly ground white pepper

If possible, use a 12-by-16-inch sheet pan with 1-inch sides. In commercial kitchen equipment, this is called a half-sheet pan. It will be the best baking sheet you may ever own if you buy from a shop selling professional equipment.

1. Use whole batch pastry made with 1-lb. flour. Roll chilled pastry on a lightly floured flat surface to a large thin rectangle, about 24-by-18 inches. Roll pastry loosely around rolling pin and unroll it over baking sheet. Carefully press pastry into edges of pan. Use scissors to trim sides evenly, leaving ½-inch pastry above edges of pan. Trim will weigh at least 6 oz. Fold over cut edge toward inside of pan. Use your fingers to crimp decorative edge. Chill pastry overnight or at least 1 hour.

2. Preheat oven to 400°F. Line interior of pastry shell with foil. Fill with ½ inch baking beans, pressing beans into corners, and bake 25–30 minutes or until pastry is fully set and begins to look cooked on inside.

3. While pastry is baking, pour defrosted spinach into strainer and press out excess water. Mix spinach with onion and garlic. Season to taste with salt, freshly ground white pepper, freshly grated nutmeg, dill. Gather all filling ingredients near oven.

4. When pastry is half-cooked, remove from oven and lift out foil and beans. Check bottom and sides of pastry to make sure there are no cracks. If there are small cracks, flatten a small ball of extra pastry between your thumb and fingertips. Daub pastry patch with a little egg white using a fingertip and lay patch over crack. Sprinkle bottom of warm pastry with grated cheese. Distribute spinach mixture evenly over cheese, using your fingertips to feather it evenly. Use a ladle to gently pour in quiche filling, moving ladle back and forth across spinach filling until pastry crust is almost full. Use rubber spatula to smooth top. (Do not fill shell entirely to top, or you may have trouble getting it back into oven.)

5. Return quiche to hot oven and continue to bake 40–45 minutes or until custard is puffed and golden. Remove quiche from oven and allow to cool on wire rack. For easy removal from baking pan, quiche will need to be lukewarm. Cold pastry will stick to bottom of pan.

6. To remove quiche from pan, place large wire rack or cutting board over top of quiche. Flip quiche over as you hold two ends of pan. Once quiche is upside-down on rack or board, lift off baking pan. Place second cutting board over bottom of quiche and flip it over again. Quiche will be upright on cutting board.

7. To cut quiche into 80 mini-portions, use a thin, sharp, or serrated knife. Cut quiche in half both lengthwise and crosswise. Cut each quarter into 20 small squares by making 4 lengthwise cuts and 5 crosswise cuts. Repeat this process with other 3 rectangles. Arrange 80 squares on large serving platter. Garnish with fresh herbs and flowers.

FRESH TOMATO PIZZA

At the height of summer's tomato season, when there's a day cool enough to turn on the oven, splurge on this baked cousin to Panzanella. Serve it in small rectangles with drinks or in big wedges with a salad for supper.

1 lb. French Bread dough (p. 96)
2½–3 lbs. fresh ripe tomatoes (from garden or farmers' market)
4–5 tablespoons olive oil
1 tablespoon finely chopped garlic
½ teaspoon finely chopped fresh red chili (optional)
1 oz. (1 cup loosely packed) fresh basil leaves, sliced
1 oz. (¼ cup) grated Parmesan cheese
3 oz. (¾ cup) grated whole milk mozzarella, white Cheddar, or Swiss cheese
salt and freshly ground pepper

1. While dough is rising, scald tomatoes 10 seconds in boiling water. When tomatoes are cool, pull off skins, core, and slice into ¼-inch circles. Spread tomatoes on baking sheet; sprinkle with salt and allow to stand at least 30 minutes to draw out excess water.

2. Place strainer over bowl and scrape tomatoes into strainer. Shake out juice from tomatoes (be sure to save juice for soup). There should be 3–3½ cups drained tomato and 12 fl. oz. (1½ cups) juice.

3. Gently sweat garlic and chili in 1 tablespoon olive oil until softened; cool to room temperature. Coarsely cut basil.

4. When bread dough is ready to shape into loaves, measure off 1 lb. or approximately ⅖ of batch. (Shape remainder into 8 or 9 large rolls or 2 baguettes.) Roll dough for pizza on lightly floured flat surface to 14-inch circle. Place circle on cornmeal-dusted round pizza pan or large baking sheet. If dough has a tendency to spring back, let it rest and push out edges with your fingertips. Allow dough circle to rise 20–30 minutes.

5. Preheat oven to 450°F. When dough looks puffed and risen, coat top with 1 tablespoon olive oil; spread over garlic and chili. Strew over basil and grated cheeses. Lay tomato slices close together in concentric circles until entire top of pizza is covered except for half-inch border at edge. Sprinkle with generous grinding of black pepper. Drizzle tomatoes with 3 tablespoons olive oil. Bake 20–30 minutes or until crust is golden and tomatoes are shriveled. Makes one 14-inch pizza, which may be cut into 6 large wedges or 16–25 cocktail bits. (Believe it or not, this pizza may be frozen and reheated for party food. To reheat place whole pizza directly on oven rack and bake in 350°F oven until hot and crisp on bottom.)

MINI BAKED SPUDS

The simplest of finger foods: baked potatoes with sour cream.

small red potatoes (B size or smaller)
olive oil
salt and pepper
sour cream
finely chopped chives or green onion
(caviar for a special occasion)

1. Wash and dry potatoes. If they are bite-sized (about 1½ inches diameter), simply shave off a little from one end, so they will not roll. If they are larger, cut potatoes in half around middle. Use a melon baller to scoop out an indentation in round top of potato. Place potatoes and balls in bowl and coat generously with olive oil; sprinkle with salt and pepper. Place oiled potatoes on baking sheet, flat side down, indented side up—bake scooped balls alongside for yourself. Bake in preheated 350–400°F oven until potatoes are soft, 45–50 minutes. Squeeze potatoes gently to make sure all are well cooked, but do not allow them to dry out.

2. Cool potatoes until easy to handle. Place ½ teaspoon sour cream in each indentation. (Top with tiny bit of caviar, optional.) Place potatoes on serving platter and sprinkle generously with finely chopped chives or green onion; dust with coarsely ground pepper.

Note: Potatoes may be served warm or at room temperature, but they should not be refrigerated before serving. They will harden and lose flavor when chilled.

Finger Food Notes

DESSERTS

Mary Jo's was never the place to skip dessert. I began as a baker. I'd made wedding cakes for years and kept French pastry technique alive in my hands. The homemade goodness of our cakes, pies, puddings, and ice creams comforted everyone.

BREAD PUDDING WITH CRÈME ANGLAISE

Bread pudding was the one dessert we could not take off the menu. When I first began baking bread pudding to put some of our fabulous bread to another use, I baked it in a common Pyrex dish. It didn't sell, though it was ultimate comfort food. When we changed the shape and baked the mixture in individual round custard cups, it was a smash hit. A little round cake, the personal pud — everyone wanted it. Served warm with a light custard sauce, bread pudding was the restaurant's best-selling dessert. It's quick to put together, versatile, and inexpensive.

12 oz. loaf good French bread, sliced and cut into ½-inch cubes (9 cups)
4 eggs
6 oz. (¾ cup + 1 tablespoon) sugar
1 teaspoon vanilla
1 tablespoon dark rum or bourbon
knife-point ground cinnamon
8 fl. oz. (1 cup) heavy cream
16 fl. oz. (2 cups) whole milk
fruit of choice, 1-2 cups
cinnamon sugar for sprinkling

1. In deep bowl whisk eggs with sugar, vanilla, rum, and cinnamon. Blend in cream and milk. Add bread cubes and fold in until thoroughly moistened. Cover with plastic wrap and refrigerate overnight to allow bread to absorb all custard.

2. Next day preheat oven to 350°F. Fold in 1–2 cups fruit (see Suggested Fruit Additions p.185), and divide pudding among 10–14 individual custard cups; dust tops with cinnamon sugar. Place cups in water bath (a deep baking pan filled with ½ inch boiling water). Set water bath in oven and bake for 20–25 minutes or until puds are puffed and golden.

3. Remove cups from water bath; serve warm, or cool and refrigerate. To reheat, custard cups may be flashed in microwave for a few seconds. Use rubber spatula to scoop warm pud out of custard cup onto dessert plate pooled with crème anglaise (recipe follows). Surround each pudding with a few berries, or a drizzle of raspberry purée (p. 221) if desired. Serves 10–14.

Suggested Fruit Additions: Cider poached diced apples, frozen or fresh blueberries, sliced fresh strawberries, diced poached pears, fresh peaches, diced banana, fresh or frozen black berries or raspberries, crushed pineapple, diced dried apricots, raisins, currants, cooked sweetened cranberry (because cranberry will change pud color, place a spoonful in middle of each individual unbaked pudding).

CRÈME ANGLAISE

I think I've made enough crème anglaise to fill a swimming pool. Each batch followed this recipe, one quart at a time. Many of our guests preferred it to ice cream; John often asked for a pint to take home.

22 fl. oz. (2¾ cups) whole milk
4 large or extra-large egg yolks (freeze and save whites for meringue)
2 oz. (scant ⅓ cup) sugar
1 teaspoon vanilla

1. Heat milk in 2-quart saucepan. In medium bowl, whisk egg yolks with sugar. When milk is very hot, but not boiling, whisk ⅓ milk into egg yolks. Whisk and return milk and yolk mixture to remaining hot milk. Exchange whisk for metal or wooden spoon, and stir custard constantly in a figure-eight motion until it coats back of spoon. Test by drawing finger through custard on spoon; it should leave a definite trail. (As custard cooks, you will notice the fine netting of foam on top develop into a web of larger bubbles on the surface.)

2. When custard is ready, immediately pour it back into mixing bowl to cool, stirring from time to time to prevent a skin from forming. When custard has cooled to room temperature, add vanilla. Pour into glass jar and refrigerate. Makes 3 generous cups. Delicious with puddings, fruit tarts, cakes, or fresh berries.

CRÈME CARAMEL

Crème Caramel is surely the most internationally favored dessert. It's another perfect match for spring berries, sweet winter oranges, or autumn's poached plums. Every cook has special hints for caramelizing sugar. First on my list is the pan. I use a seven-by-two-inch heavy aluminum sauté pan purchased forty-some years ago from the original Chicago Crate and Barrel when it was just a storefront filled with shipping crates and barrels. Buckets of white sugar have been transformed into amber caramel in this now beaten, bent, and hallowed pan whose only function is to melt sugar.

Second, I use the dry-melt method, and my only little trick is to add a pinch of salt, which is supposed to hasten the melting. I do not stir the sugar, but as it begins to melt, I tilt the pan from side to side to encourage even heat distribution. The sugar never crystallizes this way, but it is very easy to let the sugar go too far. Then the only recourse is to run the smoking pan out to the woods in back, dump the molten caramel on the dirt, wash the pan and start over. Keep the heat moderate; don't answer the phone when making caramel, and you're bound for success.

A little flavoring secret in these sweet puddings is the grated orange rind rubbed into the sugar and then strained out of the custard, leaving behind its lovely infusion. This recipe uses whole eggs, and farm-fresh free-range eggs really shine here. Whenever we had extra free-range eggs, tray after tray of these exquisite custards brightened our cold case.

THE CARAMEL

Have ready 10 5–6 oz. custard cups or ramekins. Place cups on baking sheet and warm in very low oven. Warm cups will be easier to line with caramel. This amount of caramel is more than needed to line cups; however, it will provide extra for a caramel sauce to add when custards are served.

Place 7 oz. (1 cup) granulated sugar and pinch of salt in heavy shallow saucepan on moderately high heat. In 2–3 minutes sugar will begin to melt around edges. Tilt pan slightly from side to side until all sugar has become a deep amber liquid. Turn off heat before caramel reaches chestnut color; it will continue to darken in hot pan. (If you feel sugar has gone just a bit too far, plunge bottom of saucepan into bowl of cold water.) Holding caramel pan in one hand near tray of warm custard cups, spoon liquid caramel into bottom of cup. Immediately tilt cup to totally coat bottom with a thin layer of caramel. Go on to next cup until all have been lined with caramel. Add cup of water to caramel pan and cook to a syrup. Set aside. You may hear splintering sounds as caramel cools in lined cups.

The Custard

4 fl. oz. (½ cup) heavy cream
20 fl. oz. (2½ cups) whole milk
3¾ oz. sugar (10 tablespoons)
grated rind 1 medium orange
5 free-range eggs
1 teaspoon vanilla

1. Preheat oven to 325°F. Have ready a kettle of water near the boil, and a shallow roasting pan filled with caramel-lined cups.

2. Place cream and milk in medium saucepan and heat to scald. Meanwhile, grate orange rind over sugar in mixing bowl. Rub orange zest into sugar with fingertips until sugar looks orange.

3. Whisk eggs into sugar, beating thoroughly. Gradually pour very hot milk and cream into egg mixture, whisking all the time. Reverse custard mixture back into saucepan through a strainer to remove specks of orange peel. Add vanilla and ladle 4 oz. (½ cup) custard into each caramel-lined cup.

4. Add ¾-inch boiling water to roasting pan and set water bath in preheated oven. Bake custards 25 minutes or until slightly puffed at edges, still jiggly in center, and when a damp sharp paring knife inserted in center comes out clean. Immediately remove custard cups from water bath. Allow to cool on wire rack and refrigerate overnight before serving.

To serve, run a sharp knife around the edge of each custard cup and reverse on a serving plate. If custard does not shake out of cup with ease, twist it a bit with your fingertips as you hold the cup upside-down over the plate.

Caramel should have melted to form a light surrounding liquid. Drizzle over a bit more caramel syrup if desired and surround the pudding with sliced strawberries, orange segments, or pieces of poached rhubarb. Serves 10.

CARROT CAKE

For busy weekends, catered events, and receptions, carrot cake was the top choice. It keeps well and always pleases. This recipe includes a luscious caramel filling and a tart lemon icing, which are welcome changes from the usual heavy cream cheese frosting. A 10-inch layer cake will make 20 servings.

3 oz. (½ cup) tinned, crushed pineapple puréed in blender
1 lb. carrots, peeled and grated (4 cups) (food processor works here)
4 eggs
14 oz. (2 cups) sugar
6 fl. oz. (¾ cup) sunflower oil (or other vegetable oil)
10 oz. (2 cups) all-purpose flour
2 teaspoons baking powder
1 teaspoon baking soda
2 teaspoons cinnamon
½ teaspoon salt
generous grating nutmeg
5 oz. (1 cup) mixed raisins and currants
3 oz. (¾ cup) chopped walnuts or pecans

1. Thoroughly butter and flour 2 10-inch by 2-inch round cake pans or 3 8- or 9-inch by 2-inch pans. Preheat oven to 350°F.

2. Sift together flour, baking powder, soda, cinnamon, salt, nutmeg, and set aside.

3. In deep mixing bowl beat eggs; gradually add sugar, beating until thick and light. Slowly pour in oil beating to emulsify. Remove bowl from mixer and stir in carrots, pineapple, and spiced flour. Add raisins, currants, nuts, and mix until thoroughly combined. Divide batter evenly in prepared pans and bake about 30 minutes or until cake tests done with a toothpick, and springs back to touch.

4. Remove from oven, allow to rest 5 minutes. Loosen edges and turn out on cooling rack. Top with another rack and flip over, since top of cake may stick to rack as it cools. While cake cools, prepare caramel filling.

CARAMEL PECAN FILLING

3 fl. oz. (⅓ cup) milk + 2 tablespoons flour
2 oz. (½ stick) butter
5 oz. (⅔ cup) sugar
4 fl. oz. (½ cup) heavy cream
2–3 oz. (½ cup) chopped pecans

1. Place milk and flour in blender; whiz to combine. Set aside.

2. In heavy saucepan, caramelize butter and sugar until sandy-beige. Remove from heat and add heavy cream. Stir to dissolve caramel. Simmer and thicken with milk and flour. Filling should now have cooked to 1 generous cup.

3. Cool and add chopped pecans. Sandwich layers with filling, tops facing each other. Chill cake and prepare icing.

LEMON BUTTER ICING

4 oz. soft unsalted butter (1 stick)
8 oz. powdered sugar (2 cups)
grated rind and juice of 1 medium lemon (2–3 tablespoons juice)
2 tablespoons cream if needed

Cream butter and sugar; add grated lemon rind and juice. Whip to fluffy icing. If icing seems too thick, add bit of cream.

Cake shop icing tips: Always work with cool cake. Spread a very thin layer of icing (the crumb coat) over and around entire cake and chill thoroughly before adding final coat of icing. This will give a smooth layer of icing with no cake crumbs marring the surface. Ripple the top and sides if desired with a "cake comb"; pipe a scalloped edge with a pastry bag, using a small star tube. Dust top with finely chopped pecans.

CHOCOLATE LAYER CAKE

Americans love chocolate. Nowhere else in the world does chocolate get such acclaim. I could have jewel-like fruit tarts and exquisite French cheeses on my menu, but I'd always sell more chocolate cake. After a twenty-five-year search for the right recipe, once I found this one, I stayed with it. This cake is moist, never tunnels, bakes level, and is made with cocoa. Filled with cream and glazed with ganache, this is my best chocolate layer cake.

3½ oz. (⅞ cup) Dutch processed cocoa, or plain cocoa powder
10 fl. oz. (1¼ cups) boiling water
2 fl. oz (¼ cup). milk
1 teaspoon vanilla
8½ oz. (1⅞ cups) cake flour
½ teaspoon salt
¾ teaspoon baking soda
8 oz. (2 sticks, 1 cup) very soft unsalted butter
7 oz. (1 cup packed) soft brown sugar
7 oz. (1 cup) sugar
4 eggs

1. Cut parchment circles to line bottoms of 2 10-inch by 2-inch cake pans, or 3 8- or 9-inch by 2-inch pans. Butter and flour pans, inside the edges and paper lining. Set aside; preheat oven to 325°F.

2. In small bowl whisk cocoa and boiling water to form smooth paste; add milk and vanilla. Into another bowl sift flour, salt, and baking soda.

3. In deep mixing bowl, cream butter adding both sugars (make sure you rub out any lumps in brown sugar) and whip until light. Beat in eggs, 1 at a time. Alternately blend in flour and cocoa mixtures in 3 additions. Batter will be thin.

4. Divide batter into prepared pans and bake in preheated oven 20–30 minutes or until cake pulls from sides of pan and feels springy. For the cake to remain moist as it cools, it will seem slightly undercooked; that's O.K. Allow to cool 5 minutes in pans. Turn out onto cooling racks, peel off parchment paper. Top with second rack and reverse layers, leaving cakes upright to cool.

Note: To make a smaller cake—2 8-inch layers—use 1¾ oz. cocoa (½ cup minus 1 tablespoon), 5 fl. oz. boiling water (½ cup + 2 tablespoons), 2 tablespoons milk, ½ teaspoon vanilla, 4¼ oz. cake flour (1 cup minus 1 tablespoon), ¼ teaspoon salt, ³⁄₈ teaspoon soda, 4 oz. butter (1 stick), 3½ oz. each white and brown sugars (½ cup each), 2 eggs.

CREAM FILLING

8 fl. oz. (1 cup) heavy cream
1 tablespoon sugar
½ teaspoon vanilla

Whip cream with sugar and vanilla until stiff peaks form. Sandwich cake layers, both tops facing filling, with whipped cream. Press hand around edges of cake top to ensure filling levels out to sides; even edge with palate knife. To crumb-coat cake, use some softened ganache (left from previous batch), chocolate icing (p. 195), or apricot glaze (p. 208), and spread thinly over sides and top of cake. Chill filled cake before pouring over ganache (recipe follows).

GANACHE

5 fl. oz.(½ cup + 2 tablespoons) heavy cream
1 teaspoon honey or corn syrup
6 oz. (1 cup) chopped bittersweet or semi-sweet chocolate (not chips)

In small saucepan scald cream and honey almost to boil. Remove from heat and add chocolate. Stir gently until chocolate is evenly melted. Cool slightly and pour over cold, filled layer cake, evenly spreading ganache around sides. (A turntable cake stand is helpful for this step.) Once icing begins to set, use a tart pan bottom to lift cake onto plate. Iced cake may be held at cool room temperature for an hour or chilled. To cut in even slices, use a thin knife dipped in very hot water and wiped dry. A 10-inch cake will make 20 slices.

Note: This amount of ganache will make 3 oz. more than needed for an 8-inch cake. Freeze leftovers and save to crumb-coat your next layer cake, or use for fudge sauce for ice cream, or chill and roll into balls and dust with cocoa for truffles.

VALENTINE'S DAY

Everyone wants to dine out on Valentine's Day. They are all twos, and we had only ten tables. We knew we'd have to crank and hustle for three of us to turn out fifty-four special Saturday night dinners. Pat put up her hair and donned dangling earrings. She poured extra wine and kept the house happy. Soft lights, Bach's Cello Suites, popping champagne corks, and roses filled the room with city chic.

The lovers' dinner featured shrimp bisque and mushroom soup, lamb korma, wine-braised salmon, and Moroccan lemon chicken. Romantic sweets included fresh coconut layer cake, cranberry cheesecake, and chocolate pots de crème. Everyone found scoops of homemade raspberry ice cream and tiny hand-cut heart-shaped butter cookies on their dessert plates before they walked out into the night.

Two days later my hands still trembled and my left shoulder nagged.

French Chocolate Almond Cake

There cannot be just one chocolate cake. A prize here for the rich, deep European chocolate flavor and the moist creamy texture that only ground almonds provide. Served in tiny wedges, it is the famous Queen of Sheba Cake. With a glaze of apricot or seedless raspberry jam between the cake and the icing, it becomes a Viennese torte. On Valentine's Day, serve this amazing cake with homemade Raspberry Ice Cream and Crème Anglaise.

6 oz. (1 cup) bittersweet or semi-sweet chocolate, cut in pieces (not chips)
4 oz. (1 stick) unsalted butter
3 tablespoons brandy, dark rum, or strong coffee
¼ teaspoon almond extract or 1 teaspoon vanilla (optional)
4 eggs at room temperature, separated
5¼ oz. (¾ cup) sugar
2 oz. (½ cup) ground blanched almonds*
1 oz. cake or all-purpose flour (scant ¼ cup) (for a flourless cake, increase
  ground almonds to 3 oz.)
pinch each of salt and cream of tartar (optional)

* Ground blanched almonds or almond flour may be found among packaged health foods.

1. Line with parchment circle, then butter and flour a 9- or 10-inch by 2-inch cake pan or spring form pan. Preheat oven to 325°F.

2. Place chocolate and butter in deep bowl (preferably Pyrex). Fit bowl over 3-quart saucepan half-filled with water (to make double boiler). Bring water in saucepan to simmer over moderate heat. Turn off heat and allow chocolate to melt, stirring occasionally. When chocolate is melted, stir in brandy, rum or coffee and optional almond or vanilla extract. Keep bowl over water to retain warmth.

3. While chocolate is melting, separate eggs and measure sugar. Sift together ground almonds and flour. To egg whites in mixer bowl, add 1 tablespoon sugar, pinch each of salt and cream of tartar.

4. After chocolate has melted, whisk in remaining sugar and beat in egg yolks one at a time. Beat egg whites until stiff. Carefully fold almond and flour mix into chocolate alternately with beaten egg whites. Fold steadily and smoothly, using a light touch.

5. Scrape batter into prepared cake pan. Bake in preheated oven 25–35 minutes or until slightly puffed. Test with toothpick and remove from oven when some cake bits adhere to toothpick. Cake will still feel soft in center. Chocolate cake of this type needs to be baked slightly underdone to stay moist as it cools. Remove from oven and place on wire rack. Cool cake completely in baking pan.

6. When cake is completely cool, invert on removable bottom of tart pan. Remove parchment, slide onto flat serving plate, and brush with strained, warm apricot or raspberry jam. Glaze with Ganache (p. 192) or cover with Chocolate Butter Icing (recipe follows). Serves 10–12.

Note: This cake may puff and then fall slightly with a cracked crust as it cools. If your cake cracks as it cools, level the top by pressing gently with a cardboard circle or a tart pan bottom before turning cake out of pan.

For an elaborate layer cake that will serve 20–24, double recipes for both cake and icing. Bake cake in two 10-inch layers; sandwich when cool with chocolate icing; cover top and sides with icing. Pipe icing rosettes around the edge.

CHOCOLATE BUTTER ICING

3 oz. semi-sweet or bittersweet chocolate cut in small pieces (½ cup)
1½ tablespoons dark rum, brandy, or strong coffee
3 oz. unsalted butter at room temperature (6 tablespoons)
½ teaspoon vanilla

1. Melt chocolate with rum, brandy, or coffee in Pyrex bowl placed over saucepan half-filled with water. Turn off heat when water boils. Allow chocolate to melt slowly.

2. Whisk butter into melted, warm chocolate; add vanilla and allow to stand until it reaches a spreadable consistency. Do not refrigerate. Just give it time.

LEMON LAYER CAKE

The favorite 1–2–3–4 cake in weights for baker's precision. An excellent basic yellow butter cake and a foolproof chocolate layer cake are essential for a dessert repertoire. This recipe makes a large celebration-size cake that will serve 20. The formula may be divided for 2 8-inch layers that will serve 12.

8 oz. (2 sticks) very soft unsalted butter
14 oz. (2 cups) sugar
4 large eggs—3 separated, 1 whole
1 teaspoon vanilla
12 oz. (3 spooned-in cups) cake flour
½ teaspoon salt
2 teaspoons baking powder
12½ fl. oz. (1⅓ cups) thin milk (half water)

1. Make sure all ingredients are at room temperature. Generously butter and flour 2 10-inch by 2-inch or 3 8- or 9-inch by 2-inch cake pans. Preheat oven to 350°F.

2. Sift together flour, salt and baking powder; set aside. Separate 3 eggs. Add 1 tablespoon sugar to egg whites. In deep mixing bowl, cream butter and gradually beat in remaining sugar until creamy and light. Add egg yolks and whole egg one at a time. Add vanilla. Scrape down mixing bowl. In separate bowl, whisk egg whites with sugar until satiny stiff peaks form.

3. On low mixing speed, alternately add flour and liquid (milk + water) in 4 additions to creamed mixture. Make sure each addition is thoroughly blended. Remove bowl from mixer; fold in beaten egg whites. Divide batter into prepared pans, and bake in preheated oven 25–35 minutes.

4. When cake is done, it will be golden on top, pulling away from side of pan, and a toothpick inserted in center will come out clean. Remove from oven, allow to rest 5 minutes, and turn layers out onto cooling rack. Immediately top with another rack, reverse layers, leaving cake upright to cool.

Note: For 2 8- or 9-inch layers, prepare ¾ of above recipe: 6 oz. butter (¾ cup), 10 ½ oz. sugar (1½ cups), 3 large eggs (separate 2), ¾ teaspoon vanilla, 9 oz. cake flour (2¼ cups), ⅜ teaspoon salt, 1½ teaspoon baking powder, 8 fl. oz. mixed milk and water (1 cup).

LEMON CURD

> 3 whole eggs (free range if possible)
> 2 egg yolks (freeze whites for meringues)
> 5 oz. (scant ¾ cup) sugar
> grated rind of 2 lemons
> 6 fl. oz. (¾ cup) lemon juice
> 2 oz. (½ stick) unsalted butter

Grate lemon rind over sugar and rub in with fingertips. Whisk eggs and yolks; add lemon sugar, whisking to make sure all egg white is thoroughly beaten. Stir in lemon juice. Over moderate heat, cook custard in heavy saucepan (enameled cast iron is perfect), stirring constantly with wooden spoon until cream has thickened to jam-like. It should never boil. Remove from heat and slice butter over top, thoroughly mixing it into the curd as it melts. Cool, pour into glass jar, and refrigerate. Makes 1 generous pint.

Lemon Butter Icing (p. 189)

TO ASSEMBLE CAKE

Split each cake layer in half horizontally. Spread ½ cup lemon curd between each thin layer. Stack split layers evenly and thinly crumb-coat entire cake with lemon curd. For 2 10-inch layers split, you will need the entire recipe of lemon curd. Chill cake at least 1 hour.

Prepare Lemon Butter Icing, whipping until very soft and light, adding cream if necessary. Ice cake over top and sides, rippling with cake comb if desired. Pipe rosettes around edge and decorate with spring flowers.

GARY, THE CAT

One winter night Heather noticed a tiger cat jumping from the outdoor compressor to a windowsill, throwing its body against the pane with a howl. This was no mangy stray but a well-groomed pet. It had no collar and the night was frosty.

We knocked on the window and removed the carpet scrap lodged atop the compressor, hoping the cat would leave. Monday, Tuesday, Wednesday, it was still there, leaping and crying by my kitchen window. There was no way I could have a cat in the shop. I called the city animal control — "We don't do cats." I called the Humane Society — "we don't do cats." I asked Ernst if he would like another cat.

Friday, the cat was still there. We were booked for the weekend, and Kitty had ventured onto the front window boxes, yowling behind the screens. Saturday morning when Dan came for the hens' scraps, we tried to catch the cat. Later that afternoon Dan returned with a live trap baited with poached chicken. He set the trap outside the kitchen window.

During dinner we checked the trap — no sign of Kitty. Midway through the evening Kitty was back at the windows, raking the screens with its claws, peering in at the patrons. When it jumped to the farthest window box, a student at a four-top glanced up from his plate and exclaimed, "That's my roommate's sister's cat, Gary; we've been looking for him for three weeks." Outside, the student yelled for Gary, scooped him up, and drove away.

Kitty had finally reached his ninth life.

CHEESECAKE

My old-fashioned, not too sweet, basic cheesecake developed from Paula Peck's *The Art of Fine Baking*. Delicately flavored with lemon, ginger, and vanilla, this is the perfect cheesecake to serve with strawberries, pineapple, poached rhubarb, plums, or caramelized apples. It's also excellent with a bottom layer of port-macerated currants, raisins, and diced figs. Add berries for Blackberry Cheesecake.

CHEESECAKE CRUST

3 oz. (scant ¾ cup) all-purpose flour

1 oz. (2 tablespoons) brown or white sugar

⅛ teaspoon salt

2 oz. (½ stick) unsalted butter

Note: Cheesecake crust is a basic shortbread. If you want to multiply the recipe, press remainder into a baking pan, prick with a fork, and bake alongside cheesecake crust for a pan of shortbread cookies.

To prepare crust: Preheat oven to 350°F. In medium bowl, combine flour, sugar, and salt. Slice in butter and rub ingredients together until mealy. Sprinkle mixture evenly over bottom of spring form pan. Cover with sheet of plastic wrap, and use your fingers to press into thin pastry layer. Bake in preheated oven 15–18 minutes or until golden.

Cheesecake Filling

1¼ lbs. (20 oz., 2½ cups) soft cream cheese at room temperature

grated rind 1 medium lemon

1 tablespoon lemon juice

2 tablespoons (1½ oz. fresh ginger) finely grated fresh ginger (optional)

1 teaspoon vanilla

¼ teaspoon salt

6 oz. (¾ cup + 1 tablespoon) sugar

4 eggs, room temperature, separated

2 tablespoons flour

8 fl. oz. (1 cup) heavy cream, whipped*

9- or 10-inch spring form pan

3-inch by 42-inch strip baking parchment (optional)

1. While pastry bakes, prepare Cheesecake Filling. In deep mixing bowl, combine cream cheese, grated lemon rind, lemon juice, ginger, vanilla, and salt. Using paddle beater or large wooden spoon, mix together until free of lumps. Set aside 1 tablespoon of sugar for egg whites, and slowly pour remaining sugar into cheese, beating continuously. Add egg yolks, one at a time. Scrape down sides of bowl and beat until smooth and creamy. Sift over flour and mix in.

2. In separate bowl, add reserved sugar to egg whites and beat until stiff. Scrape beaten egg whites over cheese mixture and fold in using a rubber spatula. In egg-white bowl, whisk cream until soft peaks form. Scrape whipped cream over cheese and egg-white combination. Fold all together carefully and thoroughly with rubber spatula.

3. Remove warm pastry from oven and lower heat to 325°F. Place optional 3- by 42-inch strip of baking parchment around inside edge of springform to prevent cheesecake from sticking. Turn fluffy cheese batter into prepared, warm, crust-lined spring form pan. Return to oven.

4. Bake approximately 1 hour and 15 minutes. Top should be lightly golden, and cheesecake will still be a bit jiggly. Turn off heat and allow cheesecake to stand in oven for another hour with the door ajar, propped open with a wooden spoon handle.

5. When cheesecake is cool, remove sides of spring form and loosen crust from bottom with long palate knife. Slide cheesecake onto serving tray before it is cold; carefully peel away parchment. To make neat slices of cheesecake, use a long thin hot knife. Run knife through gas flame, or over hot electric burner before making each cut. Rinse knife, dry, and continue.

* You may substitute 8 oz. sour cream for heavy cream; however, it must be whisked into cheese batter thoroughly before folding in egg whites.

Blackberry Cheesecake: Substitute ½ teaspoon ground cinnamon and 1 tablespoon bourbon or Scotch whiskey for fresh ginger, and evenly distribute 8 oz. frozen (do not defrost) or fresh blackberries over top of filling. Press berries just below surface of cake mixture before baking.

Note: In the restaurant, we didn't always make pastry crusts for cheesecake. We often had bits of shortbread and butter cookies left from other baking, and we used simple crumb crusts for cheesecake. Graham crackers are fine (see crust for Lime Snow Pie, p. 212). Crumb crust for cheesecake should be prebaked until warm and crisp before adding filling.

TIRAMISU

Another crowd pleaser for times when desserts have to be prepared a day or two ahead. Make espresso coffee if possible, use special chocolate for the shavings, and be heavy-handed with the brandy.

> 8 oz. mascarpone cheese
>
> 8 fl. oz. (1 cup) heavy cream
>
> 2 oz. (scant ⅓ cup) sugar
>
> 3–4 tablespoons brandy
>
> ½ teaspoon vanilla
>
> 2 egg whites (⅓ cup), organic or free range
>
> 1 Sponge Layer (p. 204)
>
> 5 fl. oz. (⅔ cup) espresso or strong coffee cooled to room temperature
>
> 3–4 oz. semi-sweet chocolate curls
>
> 2 teaspoons cocoa powder

1. To curl chocolate: Wrap a block of chocolate in plastic and clasp between your hands for a few minutes to warm, or warm in microwave a few seconds on low power. Unwrap and use swivel blade vegetable peeler to shave chocolate into small curls. You will need a dinner-plate full of chocolate curls for Tiramisu. Set aside.

2. Add 1 tablespoon sugar to egg whites in mixing bowl; set aside.

3. In large, wide bowl combine mascarpone, remaining sugar, 2 tablespoons brandy, vanilla, and heavy cream. Mix and whip with wide wire whisk until thickly creamy. Be careful to stop before cheese and cream stiffen, or mixture will appear lumpy.

4. Beat egg whites and sugar to stiff peaks. Fold whites into cheese mixture.

5. Add 1–2 tablespoons brandy to coffee. Split sponge layer in half horizontally.

6. Place bottom half sponge layer on flat serving plate. Drizzle cake with half brandied coffee. Spread ¼ mascarpone filling over coffee-drenched cake. Sprinkle ⅓ curled chocolate over cheese. Blob ¼ mascarpone mixture over chocolate.

Use palate knife to pull blobs together into even layer. Cover with top ½ cake, pressing down carefully. Sprinkle top of cake with remaining brandied coffee. Gently swirl remainder mascarpone filling over top of cake. Cover with thick layer of curled chocolate. Dust edges of cake very lightly with cocoa powder shaken through small fine sieve.

7. Chill overnight or several hours before serving. Makes 12 rich portions. Tiramisu may be frozen, then carefully wrapped.

Note: Often mascarpone can only be purchased in 15-oz. packages. Use ½ for a Tiramisu and freeze the other ½ until you are ready to make the dessert again, or double the recipe and freeze a whole cake if you have space. Unwrap and defrost a frozen Tiramisu overnight under refrigeration.

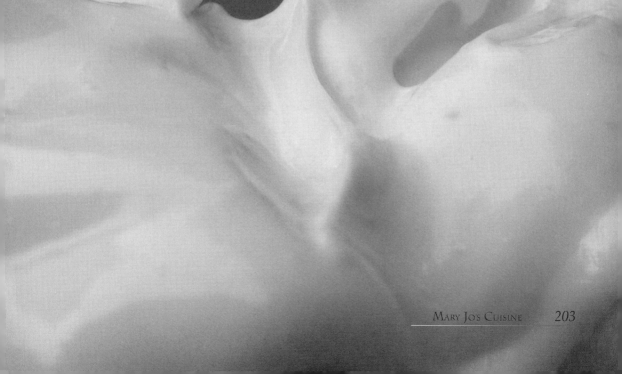

SPONGE LAYER

Instant cake, faster than a mix, only three ingredients. We kept this formula written in permanent marker on the dessert fridge door. Use it as a base for fresh berries and cream, slice and sandwich it with jam, or dust it with powdered sugar for the lightest tea cake.

> 2 large or extra-large eggs at room temperature*
>
> 3 oz. (scant ½ cup) sugar
>
> 2½ oz. cake flour or 2¼ oz. (½ cup) all-purpose flour
>
> ½ teaspoon vanilla (optional)

* For speedier whipping, immerse whole eggs in shells in bowl of warm water 10–15 minutes.

1. Butter and flour 8-inch-by-2-inch round cake pan. Preheat oven to 350°F.

2. Remove 1 tablespoon of sugar; add to flour. Sift together.

3. Beat eggs in bowl of electric mixer. Add optional vanilla. Gradually pour in remaining sugar, and whip at high speed 6–10 minutes or until eggs have risen to consistency of whipped cream, stiff enough to hold soft peaks.

4. Remove bowl from mixer. Place flour/sugar in medium sieve, and gently sift over eggs in 3 additions. Gently fold each addition into eggs using a rubber spatula. Make sure there are no flour clumps left in batter.

5. Carefully scrape batter into prepared pan and bake in middle of oven for 20 minutes or until puffed and golden.

6. Remove cake from oven. Turn cake out of pan onto cooling rack and reverse cake upright to cool.

My Apologies To The World

As hard as I try to do the right thing, sometimes I make mistakes. The last thing I intended was to make a dishonest sale. Yet one story especially haunts me: Jan often popped by for a take-out lunch, sometimes for bottles of vinaigrette, loaves of bread, or a dessert. One day early in the fall, she walked in. I had just gotten off the phone with a wine rep who had mentioned there were only two cases left of a simple but excellent 2000 Bordeaux that was going for an incredibly low $9.99 a bottle. I told Jan about the wine; she said it would be great for Christmas gifts.

Two days later when the Bordeaux arrived, I called and she drove by to pick up a case. It was a rushed Thursday afternoon, and I hadn't cleared the register from the last sale. The uncleared amount automatically added on to the wine bill, an obvious error. Unfortunately, she spotted it before I did. Red-faced, I begged her pardon, reentered her sale, and assured her I would have discovered the error that evening if not sooner. Did she believe me? I didn't know; I didn't see her again. I didn't know where life had taken her.

I apologize to the world.

APPLE CRUMBLE

As soon as the local, crisp Jonathan apples arrived at Owens' Orchard, we couldn't wait for the first apple crumble. With its crunchy, cinnamon-scented oatmeal and brown sugar topping, we served apple crumble from September through November. Throughout the winter, a box of crumble topping in the fridge meant a special dessert was at the ready. Apple Crumble is easier than pie and welcome for large family holiday dinners.

1½ lbs. (6 cups) Jonathan or other tart apples, peeled, cored, and sliced
3 tablespoons cider or water
10–12 oz. (2½–3 cups) Crumble Topping (p. 207)

Slice apples into 2-quart shallow glass or pottery baking dish. Sprinkle over cider or water. Cover with at least an even ½ inch crumble topping. Bake in preheated 350–375°F oven 30–45 minutes or until topping is golden crisp and apples are bubbling tender. (Crumble may be baked at almost any temperature; it can always go beside something else in oven.) Serves 6. If possible, serve warm with scoops of French Vanilla Ice Cream, softly whipped cream, or Crème Anglaise.

Alternatives: Add a handful or two of fresh cranberries and an extra spoonful of sugar to apples. Mix fresh or frozen blackberries with sliced apples. Try peaches or nectarines. Consider pears with a grating of fresh ginger. Crumble may be baked in a toaster oven.

CRUMBLE TOPPING

2½ oz. (½ cup) all-purpose flour
5¼ oz. (¾ cup packed) golden brown sugar
¼ teaspoon salt
¾ teaspoons cinnamon
4 oz. (1 stick) unsalted butter
4½ oz. (1½ cups) old-fashioned rolled oats

To mix in a food processor, combine flour, brown sugar, salt, and cinnamon in work bowl. Pulse to blend. Slice over cold butter and pulse to form coarse meal. Pour into mixing bowl, and rub oatmeal in with your fingertips. Refrigerate crumble mixture in sealed plastic container.

To mix by hand, combine flour, brown sugar, salt, cinnamon, and whisk to mix in bowl. Slice over butter and work in with fingertips. Add oatmeal and rub mixture together. Crumble topping will look clumpy. An alternative method is to combine all dry ingredients and to mix in melted butter. I always prefer the chunky rubbed-in version. Makes 1 lb. (4 cups).

STRAWBERRY OR RASPBERRY RHUBARB CRUMBLE

1 lb. (4 cups) rhubarb sliced
12 oz. (3 cups) strawberries sliced or raspberries
⅓ cup brown sugar
1 recipe Crumble Topping (see above)

Combine rhubarb and berries with brown sugar in 2-quart shallow glass or glazed pottery baking dish. Strew crumble topping evenly over surface and bake in preheated 375°F oven for 30–45 minutes or until fruit is bubbly and crumble is golden brown. Serve with French Vanilla Ice Cream (p. 225), whipped cream or Crème Anglaise (p. 185). Enough for 8.

Apple Tart

Everyone enjoys apple pies. A quickly baked French tart brings out the best of autumn's apples.

> 9 oz. Quiche Pastry (p. 56) (⅓ recipe)
>
> 1¾–2 lbs. tart cooking apples, 7 medium (Jonathan recommended)
>
> sprinkling of flour
>
> 2½ oz. (scant ⅓ cup) sugar
>
> 1 tablespoon butter
>
> 4–5 tablespoons apricot glaze*

1. Roll pastry to generous 12-inch circle. Fold circle in quarters, brushing off excess flour. Place pastry point in the center of a 9-inch tart pan with straight sides and removable bottom (a tart pan is shallower than a quiche pan), or use regular pie plate. Unfold pastry and press sides firmly into pan; trim overhang to an even ¼ inch. Fold overhang to inside and flute top ridge. Chill pastry shell and prepare apples.

2. Peel apples, swivel out stem and blossom ends with paring knife. Cut in half, and remove cores with teaspoon or melon baller. Place apple halves cut-side down on wooden board. Cut thin slice from both stem and blossom ends. Coarsely chop cut-off slices and set aside. Hold each apple half between thumb and first finger; cut halves into 8 or 9 ¼-inch slices. Cut through but keep slices together.

3. Preheat oven to 425°F. Dust chilled pastry shell bottom with teaspoon flour. Sprinkle over chopped apple bits. Place sliced apple halves snugly around tart shell and in center. Cut any remaining slices in half and tuck in spaces. Sprinkle apples with sugar and dot with butter. Bake tart 45–50 minutes or until pastry is richly colored and apples are brown-tinged and tender. Remove tart from oven and use back of spoon to carefully fan cooked apple slices into a circle. Brush over warm apricot glaze while tart is hot. Cool on wire rack. Serves 8. Lovely with French Vanilla Ice Cream (p. 225).

   * To prepare apricot glaze; simmer apricot jam until it has consistency of melted jelly. If jam has chunks of fruit, it will need to be strained. If jam is too sweet, sharpen with lemon juice.

STRAWBERRY RHUBARB PIE

A song of spring in itself. Wait for the fresh April rhubarb, which lifts even bland supermarket strawberries.

Pastry for 10-inch Double Crust Fruit Pie

8 oz. (1¾ cups) all-purpose flour

½ oz. (2 tablespoons) powdered sugar

⅜ teaspoon salt

5 oz. (1 stick + 2 tablespoons) cold unsalted butter

1 cold large egg beaten or ¼ cup ice water

Strawberry Rhubarb Filling

4½ oz. (²/₃ cup) sugar
2 tablespoons granulated tapioca (or 3 tablespoons flour)
⅛ teaspoon salt
18 oz. (4 cups) trimmed pink rhubarb, sliced
12 oz. (3 cups) strawberries, hulled and sliced
1 tablespoon unsalted butter
2 teaspoons cream or milk + 1 tablespoon sugar

Strip of cotton sheeting or strip of clean old T-shirt 3-by-50 inches

1. Pastry may be made by hand or in food processor. To make pastry by hand, sift flour, sugar, and salt onto a clean flat surface. Slice over cold butter and "cut" into flour with dough scraper, pastry blender, or dull knives until size of peas. Rub your fingers through flour until butter is in smaller flakes. Dribble over beaten egg or ice water, draw liquid through flour with fingers or fork, and bring dough together into compact ball.

To make pastry in food processor: Place flour, sugar, and salt in work bowl. Slice in cold butter and pulse to coarse meal. Let machine run, and pour in beaten egg or water through feed tube. Stop machine as soon as dough comes to a ball.

2. Roll dough into 5-inch log, wrap in plastic, and refrigerate overnight or at least 1 hour.

3. Divide chilled pastry in ½. Shape each ½ into 4-inch disk, and roll on lightly floured surface to generous 12-inch circle. Fold rolled dough in quarters and unfold in 10-inch glass pie plate (choose glass so you can see whether pastry is cooked on bottom). Press pastry neatly into bottom of plate and trim overhang. Add trimmings to remaining pastry dough. Dust bottom of shell with 1 teaspoon flour. Set pastry shell aside while you prepare filling. Preheat oven to 375°F.

4. In wide bowl, mix sugar, tapioca, and salt. Add prepared fruit and fold gently to combine. Scrape sugared fruit into pastry shell, and dot 1 tablespoon butter over top.

5. Roll remaining pastry to generous 12-inch circle, brush off flour, fold in quarters. Use sharp knife to make three ½-inch diagonal cuts in pastry along each fold, beginning 1½ inches from center point. (These cuts will give you 12 small steam vents—my grandma Lapp's pie design.)

6. Using your fingertips dipped in water, dampen pastry edge on lip of pie dish. Dry your fingers and unfold top pastry over fruit. Seal edges by tapping with fingertips. Trim to ¼ inch overhang. Tuck overhang under lower pastry edge; crimp as desired. Moisten strip of sheeting in cool water and squeeze out. Bandage edge of pie with cloth strip by pulling cloth around edge of pie dish half under lip and half over pastry. Overlap cloth to seal. (Cloth will protect edge from burning, will hold in bubbling juices, and will save your oven floor!) Use pastry brush to paint top crust with cream or milk and sprinkle generously with sugar.

7. Bake in preheated oven for 20 minutes. Reduce heat to 350°F and continue to bake about 40 minutes longer or until top is golden and bottom crust is evenly browned. Remove to cooling rack; peel off cloth strip while pie is still warm. Cool to lukewarm before cutting. Serve with French Vanilla (p. 225) or Lemon Ice Cream (p. 222). Makes 8–10 servings.

Lime Snow Pie

This recipe came from a *Gourmet* magazine found in a hairdresser's salon in New York City in 1963. It became my signature dessert for two years in East Africa where baking supplies were limited. Limes, condensed milk, and coconuts were plentiful, although I had to make my own graham crackers. Because this pie contains raw eggs, use only organic, free-range or farm-fresh eggs.

Crumb Crust

4 oz. (1½ cups) graham cracker crumbs (15 squares)
1 tablespoon sugar
¼ teaspoon cinnamon
2 oz. (½ stick) butter, melted
1 tablespoon honey

Lightly rub few drops flavorless vegetable oil inside 9-inch pie plate. Combine crumbs, sugar, and cinnamon. Mix honey into warm melted butter and combine with crumbs. Press mixture evenly in and up sides of pie plate. Bake crust for 15 minutes in preheated 350°F oven; allow to cool before filling. Baking the crust may be skipped; simply chill crumb crust before using. It's good either way.

FILLING

1 teaspoon lime zest

5 fl. oz. (⅔ cup) freshly squeezed lime juice (for sharper flavor
    increase to 6 fl. oz., ¾ cup)

1½ teaspoons unflavored gelatin

1 14 oz. can sweetened condensed milk (not low fat)

2 free-range eggs, washed and separated

6 fl. oz. (¾ cup) heavy cream, whipped

1 tablespoon sugar

¾ cup grated fresh coconut (optional)

1. Dissolve gelatin in ¼ cup lime juice in small cup and allow to stand until it has "sponged" or absorbed liquid. Melt gelatin by placing cup in saucepan of hot water until gelatin is clear. Hold in warm water.

2. In large mixing bowl, combine condensed milk, egg yolks, lime zest, and remaining lime juice. Whisk to combine. Gradually beat in melted hot gelatin in lime juice. Beat egg whites with 1 tablespoon sugar until stiff peaks form. Fold egg whites into cool lime mixture. Fold in whipped cream. Turn lime filling into chilled prepared crumb crust and top with grated fresh coconut if desired. Chill several hours or overnight before serving. Serves 8–10. Garnish with fresh berries.

Note: Lemon may be substituted for lime, making a Lemon Snow Pie.

LEMON TARTS

In 1982 I spent two weeks in the kitchen of a small French pastry shop in San Diego near the home of good friends. Alan was an excellent baker, but inconsistent with his budget, and the shop soon closed. These two recipes came home with me. Bake this dough into mini bite-sized pastries or individual dessert tarts.

SWEET TART PASTRY

This dough is perfect for small free-standing baked shells. It is quick to mix, easy to roll, and will not collapse when baking.

6 oz. (1½ sticks) unsalted butter, softened
4 oz. (1 loose cup) powdered sugar, sifted
½ teaspoon salt
1 large egg
12 oz. (2 and scant ½ cups) all-purpose flour

1. Cream butter and sugar. Beat in salt and egg. Stir in flour until combined. Mixture should have consistency of cookie dough. Shape dough into log. Wrap in plastic and chill several hours.

2. When ready to roll, cut off thick slice of chilled dough. Knock it gently with rolling pin to soften and roll to $1/8$-inch thickness on lightly floured smooth surface. If you have trouble rolling or if room is warm, roll pastry between 2 pieces of plastic wrap. Stamp out circles with 2½-inch round cutter, and ease pastry into small tart molds. Cut 3½-inch circles for individual tarts or roll large circles for 7- or 9-inch tart pans. Leftover pastry freezes well.

3. Chill lined tart pans on cookie sheets overnight, at least 30 minutes, or freeze 10 minutes before baking in 350°F oven 12–15 minutes, until lightly golden. Remove tart shells from molds while still warm. Baked shells may be stored in airtight tin or plastic box for several days before filling or they may be frozen.

Lemon Filling

Almost a lemon curd. Prepare the filling when ready to fill the tart shells and ladle it in hot. The filled tarts are best if used within a few hours because storage and refrigeration make them soften.

> 2 large eggs
> 1 large or 1½ small lemons (2 teaspoons zest, 4 tablespoons juice)
> 3 oz. (6½ tablespoons) sugar
> ½ oz. (1 tablespoon) unsalted butter

1. Rub lemon zest into sugar. In medium bowl, beat eggs well. Beat in sugar, lemon juice, and pour mixture into heavy saucepan, such as enameled cast iron. Cook over moderate heat, stirring constantly, until custard begins to thicken.

2. Remove from heat; stir in sliced butter. Pick out any small lumps of cooked egg white that may have surfaced, and ladle warm lemon filling immediately into baked tart shells. Mini tart shells will need 1 tablespoon filling each. If used while hot, custard will settle into shells with shiny, even surface. Cool and serve tarts straightaway or decorate later with rosettes of whipped cream and fresh raspberries. Enough filling for 17 mini tarts or 6 individual tart shells.

Note: The tarts will be at their best if used within 5 hours of filling.

MERINGUE CIRCLES

Every kitchen has extra egg whites. Whenever I make ice cream, custard sauce, or mayonnaise, I squirrel the egg whites away in a glass jar in my freezer. Once the jar is full and the humidity is low, it's time to make meringue circles or kisses. Stored in airtight tins or plastic boxes, the meringues will keep for two weeks and may be put together with simple fillings for dramatic desserts. The two I served most were Chocolate Meringue Cake and Lemon Raspberry Meringue Cake (recipes follow).

4 fl. oz. (½ cup) egg whites, room temperature
6 oz. (1¼ cups) powdered sugar

1. Line baking sheet with parchment and trace 2 8-inch circles (use cake pan or pot lid as guide). Invert parchment so pencil mark is underneath. Preheat oven to 300°F.

2. In clean mixing bowl, combine egg whites and sugar. Attach whip and beat at high speed until stiff peaks form (about 6 minutes).

3. Immediately use rubber spatula to divide meringue between 2 circles on parchment. Use palate knife to even tops and edges. Work quickly, because meringue doesn't like messing about once it is beaten.

4. Place meringues in oven and lower heat to 250°F. Bake meringue circles for 30 minutes. Lower heat to 200°F and bake for 30–60 minutes longer (may need to lengthen time if baking more than one tray of meringue circles). Turn off oven and allow meringues to dry until oven is cold. Meringues should be crisp. Store airtight.

Note: To make *Meringue Kisses* or small cookies, follow recipe for Meringue. Drop by teaspoons or pipe small rosettes on parchment-lined baking sheet. Bake as directed. Serve with fruit or ice cream. Children love these.

CHOCOLATE MERINGUE CAKE

Many were the nights I whisked this cake together minutes before locking the door. I would always be greeted the next day with sighs of approval when desserts were served for luncheon or dinner. Clouds of dark chocolate mousse and soft marshmallow-like layers of meringue create a classy dessert in minutes. Save strong breakfast coffee; use a shot of espresso or a spoonful of instant and ¼ cup boiling water. Allow the cake to rest for 8 hours before cutting.

6 oz. (1 cup chopped) best quality semisweet or bittersweet chocolate

2 fl. oz. (¼ cup) strong coffee

1 tablespoon dark rum

2 fl. oz (¼ cup) half-and-half, or whole milk

8 fl. oz (1 cup unwhipped). heavy cream* softly whipped

2 8-inch Meringue Circles (p. 216)

chocolate curls or shavings (p. 202)

1. Choose glass or stainless bowl that will comfortably fit over medium saucepan to create double boiler or bain marie. Chop chocolate and place in bowl with coffee and rum. Half fill saucepan with water, top with bowl, and bring to boil. As soon as water boils, turn off heat, and allow chocolate to melt, stirring occasionally.

2. Once chocolate has melted, stir in half-and-half. Make sure both bowl and chocolate mixture have cooled to room temperature before folding in softly whipped cream. Fold cream in thoroughly, but do not over-mix or mousse will become grainy.

3. Place one meringue circle on flat serving plate. Swirl ½ mousse on meringue. Top with second layer of meringue and gently spread remaining mousse on top. Densely cover top (leave ½-inch edge) with chocolate curls or shavings, and refrigerate overnight.

4. To serve, pipe rosettes of whipped cream around edge of meringue cake. Use hot knife when cutting cake. Makes 12 servings.

Note: Chocolate Meringue Cake will keep well for 3 days; however, it will weep if covered. Meringue Cake may be frozen, and then wrapped. It must be unwrapped and defrosted slowly under refrigeration.

* Whipping cream sold in most supermarkets in 8 oz. cartons isn't heavy cream. Look for heavy whipping cream usually sold in 16-oz. cartons. The heavier cream makes a big difference in meringue cakes.

LEMON RASPBERRY MERINGUE CAKE

The princess of all meringue cakes. The prettiness of lemon mousse ribboned with raspberry purée and the berry-dressed top of this cake make it ideal for a bridal luncheon or Grandmother's birthday. With lemon curd and raspberry purée in the fridge and meringue circles in the pantry, the cake assembly will take 20 minutes tops. Allow the cake to rest in the fridge overnight before serving.

1½ cups Lemon Curd (p. 197)

2½ tablespoons Thick Raspberry Purée (p. 221)

6 fl. oz. (¾ cup unwhipped) heavy cream, whipped

2 8-inch baked meringue circles

additional whipped cream for garnish (optional)

fresh raspberries or strawberries in season

1. To make lemon mousse, stir cold lemon curd in mixing bowl to loosen. Fold in whipped cream, which should measure 1½ cups, equal to amount of lemon curd.

2. Place one meringue circle on flat serving plate. Spread ¼ lemon mousse over meringue. Dot raspberry purée over mousse with teaspoon. Do not take purée out to edge. Gently connect dots of purée, making raspberry film on top of mousse. Dollop another ¼ mousse over raspberry purée. Gently connect dollops with palate knife, making even lemon layer. Place second meringue circle over mousse. Swirl remaining ½ mousse on top of meringue. Refrigerate cake 8 hours or overnight.

3. To serve, garnish Lemon Raspberry Meringue with rosettes of whipped cream around edge. Top each rosette with fresh raspberry or strawberry slices and strew berries alongside servings. Makes 12 slices.

Note: Lemon Raspberry Meringue will keep 2–3 days in refrigerator; however, it will weep if covered. The meringue cake may be frozen and used as an ice-cream cake, or it may be defrosted, unwrapped, overnight in refrigerator. To make a simpler Lemon Meringue omit raspberry purée.

THICK RASPBERRY PURÉE

8 oz. (scant 2 cups) fresh or frozen unsweetened raspberries
4 oz. (generous ½ cup) sugar

1. If using frozen berries, cover with sugar and allow to defrost overnight in refrigerator or in saucepan at room temperature. Combine berries and sugar. Cook over brisk heat 5–6 minutes or until thickened to jam-like consistency.

2. Push warm, cooked berries through a sieve to remove all seeds. Rub seeds in sieve and scrape all pulp into purée. Refrigerate in jam jar. Makes ½ cup.

Note: There will still be a good amount of raspberry pulp clinging to the seeds. To retrieve this pulp, place seeds and 1 cup water in blender; whiz and pass through a sieve. The seeds will be clear of all fruit, and the resulting juice may be used to poach apples for bread pudding or to mix into fruit drinks.

Lemon Ice Cream

This quick, light, and refreshing ice cream uses raw eggs; make sure they are free-range and farm-fresh. Because lemons vary in sourness, sugar may be adjusted to taste.

2 large or 3 small lemons

4½ oz. (½ cup + 2 tablespoons) sugar

2 large eggs, separated

4 fl. oz. (½ cup) heavy cream

12 fl. oz. (1½ cups) whole milk

1. Wash and dry lemons. Finely grate yellow lemon zest. Rub zest into sugar with fingertips. Squeeze juice from lemons and measure 9–10 tablespoons.

2. Gradually whisk sugar into egg yolks. Mix in lemon juice. Stir in cream and milk. With clean whisk, beat egg whites to soft peaks and fold into lemon milk base. Taste for sweetness.

3. Freeze in a small electric ice-cream machine. Makes about 1 quart.
Note: This ice cream is also successful without the cream. If the cream is omitted, increase milk to 2 cups.

RASPBERRY ICE CREAM

The simplest ice cream, this one contains berries, sugar, cream, and milk. Use fresh berries in season or good quality frozen whole unsweetened berries. The berry seeds are included in this mixture. A splendid companion for chocolate cake, butter cookies, or fresh peaches.

14 oz. (1 quart) fresh or frozen raspberries
6 oz. (¾ cup + 1 tablespoon) sugar
8 fl. oz. (1 cup) heavy cream
4 fl. oz. (½ cup) whole milk
½ teaspoon vanilla or 1 tablespoon framboise

1. Crush berries with sugar and chill until very cold. If using frozen berries, sprinkle with sugar and allow to defrost. Mix in cream, milk, and flavoring. Stir well to make sure sugar is dissolved.

2. Freeze in electric ice-cream machine and store in plastic carton in freezer. Makes generous quart.

Note: For a richer ice cream, omit the milk and use a total of 12 fl. oz. or 1 and ½ cups heavy cream.

CAPPUCCINO ICE CREAM

There's no better flavor to serve with chocolate cakes or spicy puddings. Coffee ice cream is also at home with apple tarts.

12 fl. oz. (1½ cups) whole milk
2 tablespoons instant coffee
scant ⅛ teaspoon ground cinnamon (optional)
4 egg yolks
6 oz. (¾ cup + 1 tablespoon) sugar
12 fl. oz. (1½ cups) heavy cream
1 teaspoon vanilla

1. Gently heat milk in small saucepan; add instant coffee and cinnamon.

2. In medium bowl, whisk egg yolks with sugar until creamy. Gradually whisk in half hot coffee milk. Return tempered yolk mixture to saucepan with remaining milk and cook, stirring constantly until custard lightly coats back of spoon. Pour hot custard back into mixing bowl and allow to cool to room temperature, stirring occasionally to prevent skin from forming. Cover and refrigerate until very cold.

3. Add cream and vanilla to cold custard. Freeze in small electric ice-cream machine. Pack into plastic container and harden in freezer. Makes 1 quart.
   Note: For richer coffee flavor, add ¼ teaspoon pure coffee extract or essence along with vanilla.

FRENCH VANILLA ICE CREAM

One summer I worked in the preeminent French kitchen of the Watergate Hotel in Washington, DC, where celebrity chef, Eric Ripert, was still a line cook. The only recipe that stayed with me from that venture is pastry chef Gerard's vanilla ice cream. If you can find a bottle of Tahitian vanilla, the flavor will be even better.

12 fl. oz. (1½ cups) whole milk

4 egg yolks

6 oz. (¾ cup + 1 tablespoon) sugar

12 fl. oz. (1½ cups) heavy cream

1½ teaspoons pure vanilla (Tahitian recommended)

1. Bring milk to simmer in medium saucepan. Meanwhile, whisk egg yolks and sugar thoroughly in bowl. Gradually whisk half hot milk into yolk mixture. Pour "tempered" yolks back into saucepan with remaining milk. Scrape every bit from yolk bowl into milk and whisk gently. Begin to cook custard over moderate heat. When froth appears on surface, replace whisk with wooden spoon, and stir continually until mist of fine bubbles on surface begins to disappear. Cook until custard coats back of spoon and is too hot for your pinkie finger. Watch carefully—there is a fine line between cooked custard and scrambled egg yolks.

2. As soon as custard is ready, immediately pour into yolk bowl and allow to cool to room temperature. Stir from time to time to prevent skin from forming. This process may be hurried by immersing bowl in bath of ice water. Cover and refrigerate until very cold.

3. Add cream and vanilla to cold custard. Freeze in small electric ice-cream machine. Scrape into plastic carton and store in freezer. Makes about 1 quart.

DAVID'S COOKIES

My son packed these big cookies and bananas for breakfast following early-morning high-school swim practice. He now makes them for his own children who are beginning to swim.

4 oz. (1 stick) butter softened

3 oz. (scant ½ cup) white sugar

3 oz. (½ cup not packed) soft brown sugar

¾ oz. (1 tablespoon) honey

1 egg

3 tablespoons water

3 oz. (½ cup + 2 tablespoons) all-purpose flour

¼ teaspoon salt

½ teaspoon baking soda

¼ oz. (1 tablespoon) wheat germ

5½ oz. (2 cups) rolled oats, preferably old-fashioned

3 oz. (½ cup) chocolate chips

4 oz. (generous ¾ cup) raisins

2 oz. (½ cup) chopped walnuts or pecans

1. Cream butter and sugar. Beat in egg and gradually beat in water.

2. Sift flour, salt, and soda together. Blend flour and wheat germ into creamed mixture.

3. Stir in oats, chocolate chips, raisins, and nuts.

4. For large cookies, scoop dough with 2-oz. ice-cream dipper, and place 8 cookies on 8-by-14-inch lightly greased or greased parchment-lined baking sheet. For baby David's, drop cookies by teaspoon. Using a fork dipped in water, and flatten cookies to ½-inch thickness. Large cookies should be at least 3 inches across.

5. Bake in preheated 350°F oven until golden. Large cookies will take 12–15 minutes and small cookies will bake in 10–12 minutes. Watch carefully, because honey causes cookies to darken quickly. Cool slightly before removing to wire racks. Layer with waxed paper for storage.

Makes 18 large cookies or 5–6 dozen babies.

Note: If cookies seem too fragile, add extra tablespoon flour to dough.

CATHERINE'S BISCOTTI

Crisp, flavorful, and not too sweet — perfect with coffee or dessert wine.

4 oz. (scant cup) whole unblanched almonds
6 oz. (¾ cup + 1 tablespoon) sugar
zest 1 small orange or lemon
2 oz. (½ stick) soft butter
2 eggs
1 teaspoon vanilla
⅛ teaspoon almond extract (optional)
½ teaspoon salt
1 teaspoon whole anise seeds (optional)
10 oz. (2 cups) all-purpose flour
1 teaspoon baking powder
¼ teaspoon baking soda

1. Preheat oven to 350°F and roast almonds 12–15 minutes or until very lightly browned inside and some beginning to split. Cool slightly and chop coarsely. Set aside.

2. Place sugar in mixing bowl and grate over orange or lemon zest. Work zest into sugar with your fingertips. Add soft butter and cream into sugar.
Mix in eggs and beat until smooth. Add vanilla, almond extract, salt, and anise seeds.

3. Sift flour, baking powder, and baking soda into the creamed mixture and combine. Stir in chopped almonds and turn the dough onto a lightly floured countertop. Knead briefly; cut dough into 2 equal parts. Roll each to a 14-inch-by-1½-inch log and place the logs on lightly greased or parchment lined cookie sheet. Leave 3 inches between logs. Press tops of logs down slightly with palm.

4. Bake 15–20 minutes in 350°F oven or until golden and firm. As soon as baked logs can be handled, gently lift to cutting board and while still warm slice into ½-inch diagonal cookies. Lay cookies flat on baking sheet and return to oven about 10 minutes or until lightly toasted. Allow to cool thoroughly; cookies will crisp as they cool. Store airtight in tin or plastic box. Makes 24–36.

Note: To make large café-style biscotti, shape dough into one large log 18 by 2½ inches. Place log crosswise on cookie sheet. Bake 30–35 minutes and cut into 14–16 long, diagonal pieces. Toast 12–15 minutes, turn off oven heat, and allow to cool in oven until fully dry. Leave door ajar if using electric oven.

POWDERED BALLS

Festive melt-in-your-mouth cookies. The most famous are Greek Kourabiethes. My first recipe, from a fifth-grade music teacher, was called Chinese Dreams. The theme reoccurs in Russian Tea Cakes, Mexican Wedding Cookies, and Spanish Polvorones.

Some recipes include egg yolk and baking powder. Various nuts may be used, from roasted blanched almonds or hazelnuts, to walnuts or pecans. My little secret for these cookies is the addition of a tiny drop of anise oil. Anise oil is an amazing flavor catalyst in butter cookies, but it is very strong and must be used with discretion. Anise oil is not anise extract, and may be purchased from a pharmacy or a pastry supply source. A small bottle will last a lifetime. The following recipe makes only two dozen small cookies. Because they keep well, I always make four times the given amount. The increased proportions are noted at the end of the recipe.

4 oz. (1 stick) softened unsalted butter
1 oz. (¼ cup) powdered sugar
⅛ teaspoon salt
1 tiny drop anise oil (optional)
½ teaspoon vanilla
1½ teaspoons brandy
4 oz. (1 spooned-in cup) all-purpose flour
2 oz. (½ cup) chopped pecans or blanched roasted almonds
additional powdered sugar

1. Cream butter with sugar until white and fluffy. Beat in salt, anise, vanilla, and brandy. Sift and stir in flour. Mix in nuts. Cover and allow dough to stand at least an hour or overnight at room temperature. This rest allows flour to absorb moisture. The dough is then ready to roll into balls.

2. Scrape dough onto lightly floured surface. Roll into a thick 6-inch log; cut the log in half lengthwise and then in lengthwise quarters. Cut each quarter in half and each half in thirds. There will be 24 even pieces. Roll each piece into a large cherry-sized ball. Place on parchment-lined or lightly greased baking sheet.

3. Bake cookies in preheated 325°F oven for 18–20 minutes. Cookies will be pale when cooked, but they should be lightly browned on bottom. Line cookie tin or plastic box with sheet of waxed paper. Sift layer of powdered sugar over paper. When cookies are cool enough to handle, place in neat rows on top of sugar-dusted paper. Sift generous layer of powdered sugar over cookies. Layer cookies, covering each layer with generous dusting of powdered sugar. Store airtight.

4. If you can stand the wait, hold cookies in cool place at least a week before serving for best flavor. (We started making these cookies for Christmas in early November and kept some in the fridge until Easter. They were still delicious.)

Note: After you finish cookies, save remnants of powdered sugar. It is buttery and perfumed and may be used in sweet tart pastry or next batch of cookies.

To make 8 dozen: Use 1 lb. butter, 4 oz. powdered sugar, ½ teaspoon salt, 2 drops anise oil, 2 teaspoons vanilla, 2 tablespoons brandy, 1 lb. flour, 8 oz. nuts.

CHOCOLATE FUDGE WAFERS

A perfect chocolate cookie—crisp, delicate, deep chocolate flavor.

4 oz. (²/₃ cup chopped) semisweet or bittersweet chocolate, not chips
1 oz. (1 square) unsweetened chocolate
5 oz. (1 cup scooped and leveled) all-purpose flour
¼ teaspoon salt
½ teaspoon baking soda
4 oz. (1 stick) softened unsalted butter
3½ oz. (½ cup packed) brown sugar
3½ oz. (½ cup) white sugar
1 egg
extra granulated sugar on a saucer

1. Chop chocolate and place in bowl over saucepan of boiling water. Remove saucepan from heat, allow chocolate to melt. Cool slightly.

2. Sift together flour, salt, and baking soda.

3. Cream butter with sugars; beat in egg. Scrape melted chocolate into creamed mixture. Beat to combine, and mix in dry ingredients. The mixture will seem too soft for a shaped cookie, but do not refrigerate. Let cookie dough stand at room temperature for 30–60 minutes or overnight, depending on warmth of room, until dough can be handled.

4. Preheat oven to 325°F. Scrape cookie dough onto clean, flat surface. Divide in 4 parts and shape each into long snake. Cut snake in segments and roll each into cherry-sized ball. Place balls on parchment-lined or lightly greased baking sheet (24 to a sheet). Use small glass with lightly buttered flat bottom to dip in saucer of granulated sugar and press cookie ball to flatten. Repeat procedure with each cookie, dipping glass into sugar each time—there is no need to butter the glass again.

5. Bake cookies in preheated oven about 12 minutes. Cookies may seem soft but will firm up and crisp as they cool. Remember chocolate bakes quickly. Cool on wire rack and store airtight. Makes at least 6 dozen.

Note: For ultimate chocolate sandwich cookies, join 2 Chocolate Fudge Wafers back to back with dab of Chocolate Butter Icing (p. 195) or cool Ganache (p. 192).

CANDIED GINGER CRISPS

A Christmas cookie or a tea wafer — buttery, gingery, special.

8 oz. (2 sticks) soft unsalted butter

7½ oz. (generous cup packed) light brown sugar

1 egg yolk

1 teaspoon vanilla

3 oz. (⅔ cup) finely chopped candied ginger

½ teaspoon powdered ginger

8 oz. (1¾ cups) all-purpose flour

¾ teaspoon baking powder

¼ teaspoon salt

additional sugar for sprinkling

1. Cream butter and brown sugar. Add egg yolk, vanilla, and beat until light. Stir in candied ginger. Sift in powdered ginger, flour, baking powder, and salt. Mix to combine into soft dough. Cover and allow dough to rest at room temperature until firm enough to handle.

2. Preheat oven to 350°F. Scrape cookie dough onto clean, flat surface. Divide in quarters; roll each portion into snake. Cut in cherry-sized segments; roll into balls. Place balls on parchment lined or lightly greased baking sheets, approximately 24 on a sheet. Flatten cookies with damp fork and sprinkle with granulated sugar or sugar from candied ginger.

3. Bake in preheated oven 12–14 minutes. Bang sheet on oven rack twice while baking to encourage cookies to flatten. When cookies look golden, remove to wire racks and cool. Store airtight. Makes 6 dozen.

Shanagarry Oat Cakes

If I were to choose a favorite cookie, this would be it. Rich and crumbly, from Ballymaloe Cookery School — a traditional Irish bikkie.

4 oz. (1 stick) unsalted butter, softened

2½ oz. (7 tablespoons) sugar, white or light brown

2 oz. (scant ½ cup) all-purpose flour

$^3/_8$ teaspoon baking soda

scant ½ teaspoon salt

5 oz. (1¾ cups) rolled oats, old-fashioned or quick, but not instant

egg wash, egg white, or cream and sugar for glaze

1. Cream butter and sugar. Sift in flour, baking soda, and salt. Mix well. Add oats and stir together. Allow dough to rest 10–15 minutes.

2. Scrape dough onto lightly floured, clean, flat surface. Shape into thick patty. With lightly floured rolling pin, roll to ¼-inch thickness. Cut into circles with 2-inch round cutter or cut into squares with knife. Place cut cookies on parchment-lined or lightly greased baking sheet. Reroll scraps and cut. Brush with beaten egg, egg white, or cream and sprinkle with sugar.

3. Bake in preheated 350°F oven for 10–15 minutes or until golden. Remove to cooling rack and store in airtight tin when cool. Makes 2 dozen.

Note: If the dough is difficult to roll, place it between two sheets of plastic wrap and roll as directed. This method is useful if the kitchen is warm and humid.

INDEX

A

apple
tart, 208
crumble, 206
apricot glaze, 208
asparagus
pasta salad, 29
quiche, 63
soup, 9

B

bacon and Cheddar stuffing, 120
beans Bretonne, 166
beef
Bourguignon, 112
carbonnades Flamande, 82
biscotti, Catherine's, 228
bread
crumbs, soft, 116
pudding, 184
breads and rolls
Ballymaloe brown yeast, 94
cinnamon rolls, 100
French, 96
hot cross buns, 102
scones, 98
stollen, 104
butter papers, 5
butternut squash soup, 12

C

cabbage
buttered, 153
coddled, 142
curried, 154
potato soup, 4
cakes
carrot, 188
cheese, 199
chocolate layer, 190
chocolate meringue, 218
French chocolate almond, 194
lemon layer, 196
lemon raspberry meringue, 220
meringue circles, 216
sponge layer, 204
tiramisu, 202
canapes, smoked salmon, 173
candied ginger crisps, 234
canela, xxii
cappuccino ice cream, 224
carbonnades Flamande, 82
caramel
custard, 186
pecan filling, 189
carrot(s)
cake, 188
glazed, 156
roasted, 40
soup, 8
Catherine's biscotti, 228
Ceylon cinnamon, xxii
champ, scallion, 159

S